Study Guide
to accompany

CRIMINAL JUSTICE

SEVENTH EDITION

James A. Inciardi
University of Delaware

Prepared by
Robert G. Huckabee
Indiana State University

Southwest Tennessee Community College
Gill Center Library
3833 Mountain Terrace
Memphis, TN 38127

New York   Oxford
OXFORD UNIVERSITY PRESS

Oxford University Press

Oxford   New York
Auckland Bangkok Buenos Aires Cape Town Chennai
Dar es Salaam Delhi Hong Kong Istanbul Karachi Kolkata
Kuala Lumpur Madrid Melbourne Mexico City Mumbai
Nairobi São Paulo Shanghai Taipei Tokyo Toronto

Copyright 2002 by Oxford University Press, Inc.

Published by Oxford University Press, Inc.
198 Madison Avenue, New York, New York, 10016
http://www.oup-usa.org

Oxford is a registered trademark of Oxford University Press

All rights reserved. No part of this publication may be reproduced,
stored in a retrieval system, or transmitted, in any form or by any means,
electronic, mechanical, photocopying, recording, or otherwise,
without the prior permission of Oxford University Press.

ISBN: 0-19-515554-8

Printing number: 9 8 7 6 5 4 3 2 1

Printed in the United States of America
on acid-free paper

CONTENTS

Introduction   v

Chapter 1   *"Criminal Justice" in America*   1
Chapter 2   *Crime and the Nature of Law*   5
Chapter 3   *Legal and Behavioral Aspects of Crime*   15
Chapter 4   *Criminal Statistics and the Extent of Crime*   25
Chapter 5   *The Process of Justice: An Overview*   33
Chapter 6   *Police Systems in the United States:
    History and Structure*   43
Chapter 7   *Enforcing the Law and Keeping the Peace:
    The Nature and Scope of Police Work*   53
Chapter 8   *The Law of Arrest, Search, and Seizure:
    Police and the Constitution*   65
Chapter 9   *Beyond the Limits of the Law:
    Police Crime, Corruption, and Brutality*   77
Chapter 10   *The Structure of American Courts*   87
Chapter 11   *Judges, Prosecutors, and Other Performers at the
    Bar of Justice*   97
Chapter 12   *The Business of the Court:
    From First Appearance Through Trial*   109
Chapter 13   *Sentencing, Appeal, and the Judgment of Death*   125
Chapter 14   *From Walnut Street to Alcatraz:
    The American Prison Experience*   137

Chapter 15   *Penitentiaries, Prisons, and Other Correctional Institutions: A Look Inside the Inmate World*   147
Chapter 16   *Prison Conditions and Inmate Rights*   155
Chapter 17   *Probation, Parole, and Community-Based Correction*   165
Chapter 18   *Juvenile Justice: An Overview*   177

INTRODUCTION

Welcome to the study of criminal justice! Over the next several weeks you will be exploring the system and process that we use in the United States to respond to crime in our society. The *criminal justice* system is a varied and complex series of components that work together (more or less) to accomplish common goals—goals such as maintaining order, protecting the public, and fairly administering justice when the laws are broken. The *criminal justice process* describes the numerous activities that take place throughout the system as a particular criminal case moves from the investigation of the crime through arrest, prosecution, trial, sentencing and on to the punishment (or other disposition) phase.

Professor Inciardi has written a comprehensive textbook that will take you on a detailed journey through both the system and process of criminal justice in America. I have prepared this study guide as a companion to the textbook in the hope that it will assist you to grasp the key ideas, concepts, issues, and terms used in the text.

The chapters of the study guide are organized in a standard four-section format; follow the sections in order. You will begin with the "Chapter Outline" of the respective chapter in the text. The outline highlights the main headings and subheadings and alerts you to how the chapter is organized. I suggest you spend some time reviewing the outline before you proceed. Next, you will find a listing of "Key Terms, Concepts, and Ideas" that are important to master. You are asked to provide the definitions for each of these key terms. The third section of each chapter is called "Discussion" and includes some information that will supplement and complement what you have read in the text. In some chapters there are exercises that ask you to locate information on the Internet or in your university library, and respond to questions. Some of the websites are home to federal, state, or local criminal justice agencies, while in other cases you will be directed to specific documents. In other chapters you will find scenarios that present "real world" problems for you to analyze and resolve. Finally, you will find a "Practice Exam" (complete with answers) that tests your knowledge of the text chapter.

This study guide is not intended to be a shortcut, a substitute, or a "silver bullet." It *is* intended to be a *tool to assist you in the learning process*. After almost twenty years as a college professor, I have drawn certain conclusions about how and why some students succeed and others fail in their classes. First and foremost, in order to be a successful student you *must go to class*—class attendance is critical to learning. Many professors add their own supplementary material to their lectures, so if you are not in class you miss that

v

information. You also miss out on the opportunity to ask questions and participate in classroom discussions. These interactions with your classmates and professor are all part of learning. Secondly, spend time reading and studying your text, and working with your study guide. The text covers virtually everything you could ever want to know about criminal justice in America, and the study guide is designed to reinforce the key elements presented in the text. Both the text and the study guide are excellent sources of information, but neither will do you any good sitting on a shelf untouched. Read a chapter, take notes as you go, think about the material, then read the chapter again! Learning is an active, not passive process-you have a golden opportunity here, so go ahead and take advantage of it.

Robert G. Huckabee, Ph.D.
Department of Criminology
Indiana State University

CHAPTER 1

"Criminal Justice" in America

CHAPTER OUTLINE

I. The Emergence of Criminal Justice
  A. Definition, the structure, function, and decision processes of those agencies that deal with the management of crime, the police, the courts, and corrections
    1. criminology
    2. criminal law
    3. criminal procedure
    4. constitutional law
  B. "Law and Order" and the "War on Crime"
    1. the 1960s—a decade of violence
    2. political assassinations
    3. appeals for "law and order"
    4. "nationalization" of the Bill of Rights
    5. President Johnson's "war on crime" President's Commission on Law Enforcement and Administration of Justice
  C. The President's Crime Commission
    1. *The Challenge of Crime in a Free Society*
    2. recommendations, seven specific objectives and more than 200 specific recommendations
    3. focus on the relationship between poverty and crime

D. Criminal justice as a "system"
      1. an orderly flow of managerial decision making that begins with the investigation of a criminal offense and ends with the offender's reintegration into the free community
      2. the alternate view, criminal justice as a "nonsystem"
   E. The Omnibus Crime Control and Safe Streets Act of 1968
      1. the unique place that the year 1968 holds in America
      2. the search for the "root causes" of crime
      3. provisions of the act; responses to the act
   F. The Law Enforcement Assistance Administration
      1. created to fund improvements in state criminal justice systems
      2. early criticisms—overemphasis on technology; misdirecting funds
      3. funding for criminal justice education

II. Models of Criminal Justice
   A. The Due Process Model stresses protection of procedural rights—the Warren Court
   B. The Crime Control Model emphasizes efficiency, the Burger Court

III. Key Factors in Criminal Justice Today
   A. The war on drugs
   B. Women, crime, and criminal justice
   C. The criminal justice "nonsystem"
   D. Victims and justice

IV. International and Cross-Cultural Perspectives

V. Organization of this Book

VI. Summary

REVIEW OF KEY TERMS, CONCEPTS, AND IDEAS

Write the definitions of the key terms in the space provided.

1. Burger Court—_____

2. crime control model—_____

3. criminal justice—_____

4. due process model—_____

5. law and order—_____
_____

6. Law Enforcement Assistance Administration (LEAA)—_____
_____

7. Omnibus Crime Control and Safe Streets Act—_____
_____

8. President's Commission on Law Enforcement and Administration of Justice—_____
_____

9. Warren Court—_____
_____

DISCUSSION

Criminal Justice—System or Nonsystem?

In the text, you will find a discussion of criminal justice as a system and as a nonsystem. A system is usually described as a series of interrelated components working together for a common goal. Further, a system must have the following three elements: input, process, and output. For example, an automobile engine is a system. It is made up of many individual parts (components) which all work in harmony to produce the goal of performing work (transportation). Gasoline is placed into the engine (input), the engine burns the gasoline (process), and power is expelled out of the engine (output).

The people who argue that criminal justice is a system see the police, the courts, and the correctional agencies as components that work together to fight crime. In the system model, the police provide the input (in the form of persons arrested), the courts provide the process (converting suspects into convicted criminals), and the correctional agencies provide the output (holding the convicted criminals until they are returned to society).

Other people are not so optimistic as to accept the system model as presented above. They instead see criminal justice as a nonsystem actually made up of three independent systems represented by the police, the courts, and the correctional agencies. Under the nonsystem model, each component has its own needs, problems, goals, and agendas, and not only do not work together for a common goal, but often work in opposition to each other. When you add to this the President's Commission's observation that every "village, town, county, city, and State has its own criminal justice system, and there is a Federal one as well" (p. 7), it is easy to understand why criminal justice may be better described as a nonsystem than a system.

Think about what criminal justice might be like if there were only one set of rules that governed everyone. Instead of each state having its own laws, what if there were a national law that applied equally to everyone regardless of where they lived? There would be one set of laws establishing speed limits, legal drinking age, whether there is or is not a death penalty (and for what crimes), procedures for selecting judges, the hiring of police officers, etc. There would be a national police force, a national court structure, and a national correctional agency. Would one criminal justice system be preferable to the many systems (or nonsystem) that we have now? What are the advantages and disadvantages of a single system of criminal justice? Take a few minutes and write a short essay in which you:

1. argue that criminal justice is either a system or a nonsystem (support your position).
2. discuss the advantages and disadvantages of one single criminal justice system that would govern throughout the entire country.

CHAPTER

Crime and the Nature of Law

CHAPTER OUTLINE

I. Introduction
   A. Public perceptions of crime and criminals as a product of television dramas, movies, and selected news reports
   B. Crime is a broad concept; the commonly recognized street crimes such as murder, robbery, and burglary represent only part of the crime picture
   C. Crime also includes white-collar crime, victimless crimes, and corruption
   D. Crime definitions vary from state to state and from country to country

II. The Nature of Crime
   A. Crime as drama, as sin, and as violation of natural law
   B. Crime as a social construct; the sociology of deviance; crime is not an absolute concept, but rather a definition created by persons in power and used against other persons who threaten the social order
      1. Crime and moral crusades
         a. Howard S. Becker
         b. Prohibition movement
      2. Crime and deviance; not all deviant behavior is criminal; not all criminal behavior is deviant

C. Crime as a legal construct; Paul W. Tappan legal definition of crime: Crime is an intentional act or omission in violation of criminal law (statutory and case law), committed without defense or justification, and sanctioned by the state as a felony or misdemeanor
   1. act or omission; a crime may be something that a person does (robbery) or something that a person does not do which is required by law (misprision of felony)
   2. criminal intent, *mens rea* or the guilty mind
      a. specific
      b. general
      c. vicarious liability
   3. violation of criminal law, deals with offenses committed against the safety and order of the state (society as a whole)
      a. civil law deals with private rights and liberties and the resolution of conflicts between individuals
      b. types of criminal law; statutory law, case law, common law
   4. defense or justification, either the accused did not have intent or that the behavior should be overlooked or forgiven
      a. defense; allows a person to be excused from criminal responsibility or mitigates (reduces the severity of) the criminal responsibility, examples include insanity, mistake of fact, and duress
      b. justification; a cause or excuse for the commission of an act which would otherwise be a crime
   5. sanctioned by the state
      a. there can be no crime without a punishment
      b. the law must be specific
      c. only the offender can be punished
   6. felonies and misdemeanors
      a. *mala in se* and *mala prohibita*
      b. felony and misdemeanor, distinguished by severity of penalty

III. Criminal Law
   A. Definitions of law
   B. Origins of law
   C. The English Common Law; based on customs and common practices; provides the foundation and basic principles of the U.S. legal system
   D. Early American law
   E. Other sources of criminal law
      1. U.S. Constitution and state constitutions
      2. federal and state statutes (statutory law)
      3. administrative law

IV. Theories of Crime Causation
   A. The criminologists "stone"—why do some people, but not others, commit crimes?
   B. Biological theories
      1. criminal anthropology
      2. heredity

3. constitutional inferiority and body types
4. aberrant chromosomes
5. crime and human nature
C. Sociocultural theories
1. anomie
2. labeling
a. primary deviation
b. secondary deviation
3. cultural learning
a. University of Chicago sociology
b. Sutherland and differential association
D. Culture conflict and crime
1. Sellin—norms, values, and goal orientations in conflict with law
2. Cohen—delinquent subculture
3. Miller—focal concerns
4. Marx—economic and class conflict

V. Summary

REVIEW OF KEY TERMS, CONCEPTS, AND IDEAS

WRITE THE DEFINITIONS OF THE KEY TERMS IN THE SPACE PROVIDED.

1. abettor—

2. accessory before the fact—

3. accessory after the fact—

4. administrative law—

5. anomie—

6. case law—

7. civil law—

Chapter 2

8. common law—
9. conspiracy—
10. constitutional law—
11. crime—
12. criminal law—
13. defense—
14. deviance—
15. differential association—
16. Durham Rule—
17. entrapment—
18. felony—
19. labeling theory—
20. *Lambert* v. *California*—
21. *mens rea*—
22. misdemeanor—

Crime and the Nature of Law 9

23. misprision of felony—_____
_____

24. M'Naghten Rule—_____
_____

25. natural law—_____
_____

26. primary deviation—_____
_____

27. *Robinson* v. *California*—_____
_____

28. secondary deviation—_____
_____

29. statutory law—_____
_____

30. vicarious liability—_____
_____

DISCUSSION

I. In recent years, there have been a number of celebrated cases in which acts of violence committed by athletes during sports events have resulted in serious injury to another athlete. In one case, a professional hockey player intentionally struck an opponent in the face from behind with his hockey stick. The injured player suffered a concussion and was hospitalized for several days. In another instance, a college baseball pitcher intentionally threw at and hit an opposing player who was standing in the on-deck circle waiting his turn at bat. The pitcher apparently believed that the other player was "timing" his pitches to gain an advantage. The injured player lost partial vision and will not be able to play competitive baseball again. The pitcher was unsuccessfully prosecuted and later signed a contract to play professional baseball.

Do you believe that intentional injuries inflicted by athletes during ballgames should be considered criminal acts? Should players who commit these acts be prosecuted under criminal laws? If someone attacked you with a stick or other object in your front yard or at the mall parking lot, would that be a crime? What is the difference in the two situations? Why should assaultive behavior in one setting be a crime, but not in another setting? Write an essay in which you express your opinion on this issue, explaining why you feel this way.

II. The term "victimless crime" refers to certain behaviors that are legally defined as crimes, but seem to have no specific victim. In that sense, they are unlike crimes such as murder, robbery, and theft. Examples of "victimless crimes" are gambling, prostitution, drug use, and behaviors related to pornography (selling, possessing, etc.). Should such conduct be defined as crimes? Should persons who participate in these behaviors be arrested, prosecuted, and punished under the criminal law? Can a crime actually be a crime if no one is hurt by it? Can society as a whole be the victim of a crime? Explain your thoughts on the question of "victimless crimes" in a short essay.

PRACTICE EXAM

Take the following practice exam as a review of the key terms, concepts, and ideas in Chapter 2. Reward yourself with 2.5 points for each correct answer. The answers are at the end of the exam (no peeking).

MULTIPLE CHOICE

1. *Jus naturale*, or natural law,
    a. stands at the foundation of Anglo-American law.
    b. refers to perfect standards of justice.
    c. seems to be a variable and changing concept.
    d. supersedes man-made law.

2. According to sociological conceptions of deviance, which of the following statements is *not* true?
    a. Persons and social groups create crime by making rules whose infraction constitutes crime.
    b. Deviant behavior is behavior that is simply labeled as deviant by the members of a group.
    c. Deviance is a quality of an act a person commits rather than a consequence of the application of sanctions to an offender.
    d. Not all criminal behavior is deviant behavior, and not all deviant behavior is criminal behavior.

3. American criminal law is based on
    a. English common law.
    b. state and federal criminal statutes.
    c. constitutional and administrative law.
    d. all of the above.

4. Which phrase most accurately refers to criminal behavior?
    a. *mens rea*
    b. *mala in se*
    c. *mala prohibita*
    d. *nullum crimen sine poena*

5. _____ refers to the offense of concealing a felony committed by another.
    a. *Respondeat superior*
    b. Conspiracy to commit crime
    c. *Mala in se*
    d. Misprision of felony

6. Case law is law that
    a. results from court interpretations of statutory law.
    b. is passed by the legislature.
    c. is embodied in the Constitution of the United States.
    d. descends from natural law.

7. A ruling handed down by the U.S. Supreme Court would be an example of
    a. statutory law.
    b. administrative law.
    c. case law.
    d. jurisdictional law.

8. _____ as a defense against crime, involves "any erroneous conviction of fact or circumstance resulting in some act that would not otherwise have been undertaken."
    a. Ignorance of the law
    b. Duress and consent
    c. Mistake of fact
    d. Mistake of law

9. The shooting of an armed robber by a police officer would generally be called
    a. excusable homicide.
    b. justifiable homicide.
    c. self-defense.
    d. police misconduct.

10. Offenses designated as less serious than misdemeanors
    a. are called felonies.
    b. are called misdemeanors.
    c. are called infractions or violations.
    d. are not considered crimes.

11. Your neighbor is arrested, convicted, and sentenced to a term of 50 years in a state prison. He has been convicted of a
    a. consentable crime.
    b. treasonable offense.
    c. felony.
    d. administrative code violation.

12. The _____ represents an exception to the requirement that criminal intent must be present for an act to be a crime.
    a. Durham Rule
    b. misprision of felony rule
    c. vicarious liability doctrine
    d. *defensus interruptus* petition

13. Burglary involves the element or elements of
    a. unlawful entry of a building or premises.
    b. unlawful entry plus the intent to steal.
    c. unlawful entry plus the intent to commit a crime.
    d. unlawful entry plus the commission of larceny, rape, or some other felony.

14. _____ deals with actions committed against the safety and order of the State.
    a. Criminal law
    b. Civil law
    c. Administrative law
    d. Constitutional law

15. Crimes which are considered inherently evil and immoral in nature, such as murder, rape, and theft, are referred to as
    a. *mala prohibita.*
    b. *mens rea.*
    c. *mala in se.*
    d. misprision of felony.

16. A person is induced to commit a crime that he or she would not have otherwise contemplated but did so on the urging of a police officer. This constitutes a case of
    a. victim consent.
    b. entrapment.
    c. mistake and ignorance of the law.
    d. duress.

17. The necessity defense has been held to be a legitimate defense in the instance of
    a. escaping from prison to avoid sexual attack or death.
    b. sniffing cocaine for the drug's pain-killing effects.
    c. a citizen shooting a fleeing felon.
    d. all of the above.

18. _____ refers to customs, traditions, judicial decisions, and other materials that guide courts in decision making but that have not been enacted by the legislatures into statutes.
    a. Administrative law
    b. Case law
    c. Common law
    d. Civil law

19. Which of the following definitions of crime offered by lawyer and sociologist Paul W. Tappan is the accepted definition in the text?
    a. "The essential characteristic of crime is that it is behavior which is prohibited by the state and against which the state may react."
    b. "Crime is an intentional act of omission in violation of criminal law (statutory and case law) committed without defense or justification and sanctioned by the state as a felony or misdemeanor."
    c. "Crime is a positive or negative act in violation of the penal law; an offense against the state."
    d. "Crime is a violation of the criminal law."

20. In criminal proceedings, insanity is a _____ concept, rather than a medical concept.
    a. psychiatric
    b. sociological
    c. judicial
    d. legal

TRUE/FALSE

21. In Comanche society, the only "crime" was incest, because it threatened the stability of the family.

22. The first known written legal document, which dates back to perhaps 1900 B.C., was known as the Code of Hammurabi.

23. The Eighteenth Amendment to the Constitution of the United States prohibited the search and seizure of private property in the absence of a legal search warrant.

24. American criminal law is based on English common law, state and federal criminal statutes, and constitutional and administrative law.

25. In *Lambert* v. *California*, the matter under argument was mistake of fact.

26. Legislatures have made conspiracy a *separate* offense because they perceive collective criminal activity to be a greater risk than individual actions.

27. Criminal intent involves a person's awareness of what is right and wrong under the law.

28. Studies have demonstrated that the insanity plea is used in less than 1 percent of serious criminal cases.

29. Civil law deals with principles that determine private rights and liabilities.

30. The "zero tolerance" drug control policy allowed the federal government to confiscate any type of plane, vessel, or vehicle that was found to be transporting illegal drugs.

14 Chapter 2

FILL IN THE BLANK

31. Although its meaning may vary from one culture to the next, _____ appears to be an almost universal taboo.

32. _____ is the term that refers to criminal intent.

33. _____ is present when one can gather from the circumstances of the crime that the offender must have desired the prohibited result.

34. In _____ the U.S. Supreme Court reversed a lower court decision on the grounds that offenses such as "being addicted to the use of narcotics" were unconstitutional and that imprisonment for such an offense was "cruel and unusual punishment in violation of the Eighth Amendment to the Constitution."

35. _____ law deals with actions committed against the safety and order of the state.

36. Acts are considered to be *mala* _____ when they are not necessarily wrong in themselves.

37. _____ law embodies the legal rules and principles that define the nature and limits of governmental power, and the duties and rights of individuals in relation to the state.

38. The doctrine of vicarious liability is referred to in some jurisdictions as _____.

39. _____ generally refers to principles that determine what is right or wrong according to some higher power.

40. _____ is best defined as concert in criminal purpose.

ANSWERS TO THE PRACTICE EXAM

1. c	15. c	29. T
2. c	16. b	30. T
3. d	17. a	31. incest
4. a	18. c	32. *Mens rea*
5. d	19. b	33. Specific intent
6. a	20. d	34. *Robinson v. California*
7. c	21. F	35. Criminal
8. c	22. T	36. *prohibita*
9. b	23. F	37. Constitutional
10. c	24. T	38. *respondeat superior*
11. c	25. F	39. Natural law
12. c	26. T	40. Conspiracy
13. c	27. F	
14. a	28. T	

CHAPTER 3

Legal and Behavioral Aspects of Crime

CHAPTER OUTLINE

I. Introduction
    A. The complex nature of crime as illustrated by crime on cruise ships
    B. Crime viewed as legally prohibited conduct
    C. Crime as patterns and systems of behavior

II. Legal Categories of Crime
    A. Criminal Homicide; the killing of one human being by another
        1. murder; the felonious killing of another human being
        2. first degree murder
            a. malice aforethought
            b. deliberation
            c. premeditation
        3. second degree
            a. with malice aforethought
            b. without deliberation
            c. without premeditation
        4. felony-murder doctrine; if a death occurs during a felony, the person committing the felony can be charged with murder

Chapter 3

   5. manslaughter-unlawful killing without malice
      a. voluntary; intentional killing without malice or premeditation
      b. involuntary; unintentional death resulting from an unlawful act or negligence
B. Assault; an intentional attempt or threat to physically injure another
   1. assault and battery; an assault resulting in physical violence to a victim (the battery)
   2. aggravated assault
   3. simple assault
   4. menacing and mayhem
   5. jostling
C. Robbery; felonious taking of the money or goods of another, from that person, by threat, force, or violence
   1. requires a confrontation between offender and victim
   2. aspects of a property crime (theft) and a crime against the person (assault)
   3. specific elements
   4. degrees
D. Arson; intentionally damaging a building by starting a fire or causing an explosion
   1. problem of proving intent
   2. various criminal types
E. Burglary; unlawful entry into a structure with the intent to commit a crime
   1. breaking and entering
   2. degrees and varieties of burglary
   3. requirement of intent
   4. related statutes
F. Property offenses
   1. theft; unlawful taking, possession, or use of another's property, without the use or threat of force, and with the intent to deprive permanently
   2. various forms of theft; larceny, shoplifting, fraud, forgery, etc.
   3. larceny; the taking and carrying away of the personal property of another, with the intent to deprive permanently
   4. *Carrier's Case* and *Pear's Case*; refining the definition of larceny
   5. grand larceny (felony) and petty larceny (misdemeanor)
G. Sex offenses
   1. broad scope of illegal sexual activity
   2. rape; sexual intercourse with a female against her will and through the use or threat of force or fear
   3. statutory rape; sexual intercourse with a female under a stated legal age with or without her consent
   4. other examples include sodomy, pornography, child molesting, prostitution, etc.
H. Drug law violations
   1. various federal laws intended to ban or regulate the nonmedical use of drugs as well as the manufacture, sale, and distribution of dangerous drugs
   2. state laws vary widely and may include penalties for possession of narcotics paraphernalia (syringes and needles)

    I. Crimes against public order and safety
       1. wide range of offenses, usually misdemeanors, designed for the maintenance of public order and safety
       2. examples include disturbing the peace, public intoxication, loitering, gambling, etc.

III. Major Forms of Crimes
    A. Domestic violence
       1. broad scope
       2. battering by spouses and lovers
       3. psychological or economic abuse
       4. origins of domestic violence
       5. victim-offender relationship
       6. child abuse and molestation
    B. Hate crime
       1. definition: offenses motivated by hatred
       2. historical and global dimensions
       3. accurate counts are difficult to obtain
       4. victims: racial and religious minorities; gays
    C. Organized crime
       1. activities directed toward economic gain through unlawful means
       2. typically pursued as an occupational career
       3. long-term commitment and lifestyle
       4. commonly associated with ethnic groups: Italians, Asians, Russians, and others

IV. Summary

REVIEW OF KEY TERMS, CONCEPTS, AND IDEAS

Write the definitions of the key terms in the space provided.

1. arson—

2. assault—

3. assault and battery—

4. breaking and entering—

5. *Carrier's Case*—

18 Chapter 3

6. deliberation—

7. domestic violence—

8. felony—

9. hate crime—

10. homicide—

11. larceny—

12. malice aforethought—

13. manslaughter—

14. murder—

15. organized crime—

16. *Pear's Case*—

17. premeditation—

18. rape—

19. robbery—

20. theft—

DISCUSSION

Examining Criminal Statutes

A. Go to the library or look on the Internet for your state's criminal code. The criminal code is the body of statutory law, written by the legislature, which defines crimes and the punishments for those crimes. Write the definitions of the following crimes, according to your state's criminal code, in the space provided. Cite the provision (title, chapter, section) of the code for each definition. Specifically, note how each crime definition deals with the issue of malice aforethought, premeditation, or intent.

Larceny (or theft)-

Robbery-

Prostitution-

Assault and/or battery-

B. Does your state have a hate crime law? If so, how is hate crime defined? Write the definition in the space provided and give the citation for this law.

C. Does your state have a law that specifically defines domestic violence as a crime separate from crimes such as assault and battery? If so, write the definition in the space provided and give the citation for the law.

D. In your state, is it rape if a man forces his wife to have sex against her will? Should such an act be a crime?

E. In your state, can a man be the victim of rape? Should rape laws include men as victims? Write your state's legal definition of rape in the space provided and give the criminal code citation.

20 Chapter 3

PRACTICE EXAM

Take the following practice exam as a study aid to help you reinforce the material presented in Chapter 3.

MULTIPLE CHOICE

1. Mrs. Jones returns home early from work one afternoon only to find her husband sexually embracing the widow next door. Mrs. Jones goes into a blind rage, takes from her purse a handgun that she carried for protection, and shoots her husband to death. Mrs. Jones would most likely be charged with
    a. murder in the first degree.
    b. murder in the second degree.
    c. manslaughter.
    d. excusable homicide.

2. In the previous question, Mrs. Jones would have been charged in that way because of the presence of
    a. malice aforethought.
    b. malice aforethought and deliberation.
    c. deliberation and premeditation.
    d. malice aforethought, premeditation, and deliberation.

3. A trio of thugs holds up a liquor store. Two of them are armed. The police arrive, there is a shootout, and a police officer is killed. All three are arrested. With respect to the killing, the unarmed robber can be charged with
    a. conspiracy and reckless endangerment.
    b. assault.
    c. murder.
    d. being an accessory before the fact.

4. In the question above, the unarmed robber would be charged under the _____ doctrine.
    a. misprision of felony
    b. *respondeat superior*
    c. felony-murder
    d. conspiracy to commit crime

5. Mr. Smith is drinking heavily at a local pub and becomes annoyed by the loud talking of a man at the next table. They have words, and a fight ensues. During the altercation, Mr. Smith hits his adversary a bit too hard, and the man dies of a brain hemorrhage. Mr. Smith is likely to be charged with
    a. murder in the first degree.
    b. aggravated assault.
    c. voluntary manslaughter.
    d. involuntary manslaughter.

6. Mr. Smith in the question above then leaves the pub and begins to drive home. By this time he is quite drunk. As he approaches an intersection, he fails to get his foot on the brake quickly enough and runs down and kills a pedestrian. In this instance, although driving while intoxicated is a possible charge, he ultimately gets charged with
   a. murder in the second degree.
   b. involuntary manslaughter.
   c. voluntary manslaughter.
   d. felony-murder.

7. Assault involves
   a. an intentional attempt or threat to physically injure another person.
   b. the infliction of an injury with malice aforethought.
   c. the touching of a person with an instrument or part of the body with the intent to commit harm.
   d. any nonfatal violent attack.

8. _____ refers to assaultive attacks that result in the disfigurement or permanent disability of the victim.
   a. Aggressive assault
   b. Menacing
   c. Jostling
   d. Mayhem

9. Arson
   a. is a felony in all jurisdictions.
   b. is limited to the malicious burning of a dwelling of another person.
   c. does not apply to unimproved property (such as an empty lot).
   d. does not apply to malicious explosions.

10. In burglary
    a. the "breaking" aspect must be forcible.
    b. the entry need not be for some criminal purpose.
    c. the entry must be forcible.
    d. all of the above.
    e. none of the above.

11. The doctrine of "breaking bulk" was an outgrowth of
    a. *Pear's Case.*
    b. asportation.
    c. *Carrier's Case.*
    d. *Commonwealth* v. *Redline.*

12. Which criterion is normally used in the various states to distinguish "grand larceny" from "petty larceny"?
    a. the time when an object was appropriated
    b. the place from which an object was appropriated
    c. the value of the object appropriated
    d. the size of the object appropriated

13. Rape is the unlawful _____ of a female without her consent and against her will.
    a. carnal knowledge
    b. sexual abuse
    c. seduction
    d. fornication

14. The _____ was the first piece of federal legislation that targeted the distribution of what were considered "dangerous drugs."
    a. Controlled Substances Act
    b. Harrison Act
    c. Marijuana Tax Act
    d. Pure Food and Drug Act

15. In violent personal crime,
    a. the violence is directed against a specific victim.
    b. the violence is generally a group activity.
    c. most offenders have long criminal records.
    d. the crimes are generally of the "stranger-to-stranger" type.

16. In cases of child abuse, the offenders are generally
    a. single elderly men.
    b. parents and guardians.
    c. strangers with sex offense histories.
    d. all of the above.

17. With respect to occasional property offenders, which of the following statements is most accurate?
    a. They are generally acquainted with criminal subcultures.
    b. Their techniques for committing crimes are usually well developed.
    c. They have little or no access to structured mechanisms for the disposal of stolen property.
    d. Their crimes are generally well planned.

18. Occasional property crime
    a. is limited nonviolent petty theft.
    b. includes some robberies and armed holdups as well as instances of burglary and other thefts.
    c. is undertaken regularly and frequently, although rather crudely, by the offenders involved.
    d. is committed by members of urban criminal cultures.

19. White-collar criminals
    a. are generally businessmen who have weekend careers in armed robberies and other "heavy" rackets.
    b. have a criminal self-concept which helps to shape their philosophies about victimizing the public.
    c. approach their offensive behavior as a chosen career.
    d. rationalize their behaviors as sharp business practices.

20. Losses through white-collar and corporate crime
    a. are almost always rather small, but during the course of the year approach the nationwide total of all bank robberies.
    b. have been estimated to be tens of billions of dollars annually.
    c. are concentrated in the financial sector where embezzlements, stock manipulations, and similar dealings are quite common.
    d. are primarily in the areas of consumer fraud and the fencing of stolen goods.

TRUE/FALSE

21. Murder in the first degree involves malice aforethought, deliberation, and premeditation.

22. Assault involves the infliction of an injury with malice aforethought.

23. In burglary, the "breaking" aspect must be forcible.

24. Crimes against public order and safety are mostly misdemeanors.

25. Edwin M. Lemert's study of "naive check forgers" found these individuals to be professional, clerical, skilled, and craft workers who were, for the most part, respectable members of their communities.

26. At the heart of what is known as organized crime are sales of illegal goods and services to customers.

27. *Asportation* is the "carrying away" aspect of larceny.

28. Professional criminals are those thieves, drug sellers, prostitutes, and racketeers who pursue crime as a vocation and way of life.

29. The Harrison Act was a revenue code designed to make narcotics transferrals a matter of record.

30. Recent studies have demonstrated that the lineage between neurological damage and prenatal crack use is weaker than previous media reports have suggested.

ANSWERS TO THE PRACTICE EXAM

1. b
2. a
3. c
4. c
5. c
6. b
7. a
8. d
9. a
10. e
11. c
12. c
13. a
14. d
15. a
16. b
17. c
18. b
19. d
20. b
21. T
22. F
23. F
24. T
25. T
26. T
27. T
28. F
29. T
30. T

CHAPTER 4

Criminal Statistics and the Extent of Crime

CHAPTER OUTLINE

I. Introduction
   A. The influence of the media in forming public attitudes about crime
   B. Differences between public perceptions and actual crime trends

II. The *Uniform Crime Reports*
   A. Need for a standardized crime counting system
   B. Voluntary system of reporting and counting crimes; compiled annually by the FBI and published as *Crime in the United States*
   C. Structure and content
      1. the time clock suggests regular distribution of crime over time intervals; misleading
      2. Part I and II offenses
      3. the Crime Index
      4. the Crime Rate; the number of Part I crimes that occur in a given place for every 100,000 persons living in that place; a standardized unit of measurement that allows comparisons to be made from place to place and from year to year
   E. The extent of crime; about 11.64 million Part I crimes known to police in 1999
   F. Reliability of estimates
      1. crime is difficult to measure; secretive in nature; many crimes are either concealed or not reported

Chapter 4

    2. reasons for not reporting; fear, lack of confidence in law enforcement; wish not to get involved
    3. crime statistics may be manipulated by criminal justice officials
    4. police may not record all crimes reported to them; may not keep accurate records
   G. The *UCR:* an evaluation
    1. crime rates are useful in indicating trends in both reported crime and arrests
    2. useful at the local level for isolating community crime trends
    3. National Incident-Based Reporting System (NIBRS); 1987; redesigned *UCR;* expanded crime coverage and more detailed information; 24 crime categories

 III. Victim Survey Research
   A. Victimization surveys as an attempt to measure crimes not reported to police and not appearing in the *UCR*
   B. Bypass the police records and directly question members of the public about their experiences with crime
   C. The National Crime Victimization Survey
    1. started in 1972; provides information about the victims of crime
    2. unreported crime is several times higher than reported crime
   D. Comparing the *UCR* and NCVS, different methods and crime definitions
    1. uses of victim surveys data
    2. weaknesses include high cost of collecting data and memory of persons being interviewed
   E. Applications and limitations of victimization surveys

 IV. Self-Reported Criminal Behavior
   A. Questioning persons about their own involvement in committing crimes
   B. Uses of self-report data
   C. Limitations include validity and reliability problems

 V. Other Sources of Data on Crime and Justice
   A. *Sourcebook of Criminal Justice Statistics* compiled by federal, state, and local agencies
   B. Drug use databases
    1. National Household Survey of Drug Abuse
    2. Monitoring the Future
    3. Arrestee Drug Abuse Monitoring (ADAM) Program

 VI. Summary

REVIEW OF KEY TERMS, CONCEPTS AND IDEAS

Write the definitions of the key words in the space provided.

  1. Arrestee Drug Abuse Monitoring (ADAM) Program—_____
_____

2. Crime Index—_____

3. crime rate—_____

4. Part I offenses—_____

5. Part II offenses—_____

6. self-reported crimes—_____

7. *Uniform Crime Reports (UCR)*—_____

8. victimization surveys—_____

DISCUSSION AND ACTIVITIES

I. The Arrestee Drug Abuse Monitoring (ADAM) Program is one of several programs operated under the authority of the National Institute of Justice. Locate the NIJ Web site at http://www.ojp.usdoj.gov/nij/, then go to ADAM. Explore the information on the site, starting with the activities given below.

   A. Find the map of the ADAM site locations, and click on the site closest to your university or hometown. Read the most recent news release. What does it say about drug use preferences in your area? What is the drug of choice among arrestees at your site? How is drug use at your site similar to and/or different from drug use at other sites around the country? How do males and females compare in terms of drug use? How do juveniles and adults compare?

   B. Go back to the NIJ programs page and explore some of the other programs such as the Crime Mapping Research Center and the National Commission on the Future of DNA evidence. Also, look at the International Center for information about global crime and criminal justice issues.

II. In recent years, doctors, nurses, and others working in the medical field have taken an increasing interest in certain aspects of crime and violence. The medical community has come to define violence not only as a criminal/legal issue, but also as a public health issue. Medical associations and organizations are now heavily involved in violence research, data collection, and publication of violence related reports. The studies conducted by medical researchers provide an alternative source of information to persons interested in the problem of violence in our society. This information, presented from the perspective of medical professionals, provides a look at crime and violence that is unfamiliar to most criminologists and criminal justice researchers. Examine the Web sites of the Centers for Disease Control and Prevention at http://www.cdc.gov/ and the American Medical Association at http://www.ama-assn.org/ to find data, reports, and other information about crime and violence.

PRACTICE EXAM

Take the following practice exam as a study aid to help you reinforce the material presented in Chapter 4.

MULTIPLE CHOICE

1. The *Uniform Crime Reports* are based on
   a. arrest records.
   b. "crimes known to the police."
   c. arrests and "crimes known to the police."
   d. arrest records and victim surveys.

2. Congress authorized the _____ to collect and compile data for the *Uniform Crime Reports*.
   a. LEAA
   b. FBI
   c. Bureau of the Census
   d. Central Intelligence Agency (CIA)

3. Which of the following is *not* a *Uniform Crime Report* Part I offense?
   a. larceny-theft
   b. burglary
   c. embezzlement
   d. motor vehicle theft

4. "Crime clocks" in the *Uniform Crime Reports* should be viewed with caution because
   a. they should not be interpreted to imply any regularity in the commission of crimes.
   b. they fail to designate victim-offender relationships.
   c. they exclude the more important Part I offenses of homicide, rape, and robbery.
   d. all of the above.

5. Which one of the following is *not* a *Uniform Crime Report* Part II offense?
   a. weapons: carrying, possessing, etc.
   b. forgery and counterfeiting
   c. arson
   d. gambling

6. The sum of all Part I offenses in the *Uniform Crime Reports* during a given period of time is known as the
   a. crime rate.
   b. crime index.
   c. crime clock.
   d. incidence of crime.

7. A crime rate, per 100,000 population, is computed as follows
   a. Total Crime Index / population × 100,000
   b. Total Crime Index / 100,000 × Population
   c. Population / 100,000 × Total Crime Index
   d. 100,000 / Total Crime Index × Population

8. If there were 13,000 Part I offenses in a population of 225,000, the crime rate would be
   a. 5.777
   b. 57.77
   c. 577.7
   d. 5777

9. If there were 22,000 crimes last year and 24,000 crimes this year, the percent change would be
   a. + 9%
   b. + 19%
   c. + 1.9%
   d. + 10%

10. *UCR* estimates are most accurate in the area of
    a. homicide.
    b. forcible rape.
    c. robbery.
    d. motor vehicle theft.

11. Errors in the *UCR*
    a. are almost universally the result of the very structure of the *UCR*.
    b. are minimal, considering the massive task involved in collecting crime statistics.
    c. come from many sources, including non-reporting by police agencies and concealment by victims.
    d. are minimal at the national level since overestimates in some areas cancel out underestimates in others.

12. Victimization survey interviewers contact households, asking whether the person questioned, or any member of his or her household
    a. has been a witness to a crime during the preceding year.
    b. has been a victim of crime during the preceding year.
    c. has committed a crime during the preceding year.
    d. has any acquaintances who were convicted of crimes during the preceding year.

13. Victimization surveys have demonstrated that
    a. *UCR* estimates are not as bad as was once thought.
    b. homicide rates are at least double those reported by the FBI.
    c. the amount of crime is probably several times that suggested by the *UCR*.
    d. in some crime categories, the actual amount of crime may sometimes be less than that reported in the *UCR*.

14. What has been the *chief* contribution of victimization surveys?
    a. They have led to the rediscovery of the victim as a more complete source of information on instances of criminal activity.
    b. They have pointed out the relative inefficiency of law enforcement agencies.
    c. They have provided needed information regarding the types of weapons used in crimes.
    d. They have provided better estimates of the age-specific cohorts that are most involved in violent crimes.

15. In survey research, _____ refers to the precision or accuracy of the instruments used to measure and record the phenomenon under study.
    a. validity
    b. reliability
    c. variance
    d. standard deviation

16. Which of the following is a limitation of victimization surveys?
    a. They are very expensive.
    b. They are dependent on the memories of victims.
    c. They are dependent on the willingness of people to answer questions.
    d. All of the above.

17. The National Crime Victimization Survey can be effective in
    a. determining which people are at greatest risk of becoming victims.
    b. determining accurate data on the incidence of homicide in the United States.
    c. determining accurate data on the incidence of police corruption.
    d. all of the above.

18. The one crime that cannot be accurately counted by a victimization survey because few occurrences will emerge in a cross-sectional study is
    a. rape.
    b. homicide.
    c. theft.
    d. none of the above.

19. According to the *UCR* data presented in the text, the most prevalent "Index" crime in the United States is
    a. burglary.
    b. forcible rape.
    c. larceny-theft.
    d. robbery.

TRUE/FALSE

20. Currently, the *Uniform Crime Reports* are the only source of information on the magnitude and trends of crime for the United States as a whole.

21. *UCR* estimates are the most accurate with respect to homicide.

22. Police agencies may over report the number of crimes in their jurisdiction because they are trying to justify requests for additional equipment and staff.

23. According to the National Crime Victimization Survey, the *major* reason why victims did not report crimes to the police was because they were fearful of reprisals.

24. In addition to the problems of validity and reliability, self-report studies can also be problematic in that those respondents who agree to answer questions in such studies may be markedly different from those who refuse.

25. Crime index data refers to the number and distribution of Part II offenses.

ANSWERS TO THE PRACTICE EXAM

1. b	10. a	19. c
2. b	11. c	20. F
3. c	12. b	21. T
4. a	13. c	22. T
5. c	14. a	23. F
6. b	15. b	24. T
7. a	16. d	25. F
8. d	17. a	
9. a	18. d	

CHAPTER 5

The Process of Justice: An Overview

CHAPTER OUTLINE

I. Introduction

II. Criminal Due Process
   A. Trial by ordeal
   B. Inquisitional (inquiry) system versus adversarial justice; due process of law
   C. The law of the land
   D. The law of the land; torture and trial by battle as due process
   E. The Bill of Rights
      1. specific provisions of the Bill of Rights
      2. early U.S. Supreme Court views
   F. The nationalization of the Bill of Rights
      1. *Barron* v. *Baltimore* emphasized that the Bill of Rights was intended to protect citizens against federal, not state or local, government
      2. Fourteenth Amendment and incorporation; do all of the provisions of the Bill of Rights now apply to state and local governments?
      3. *Hurtado* v. *California* (1884), "Incorporation" debate
      4. *Gitlow* v. *New York* (1925); U.S. Supreme Court rules that First Amendment protection of freedom of speech applies to state and local governments as well as to the federal government
      5. *Powell* v. *Alabama* (1932), the "Scottsboro Boys" case

6. *Palko* v. *Connecticut* (1937); U.S. Supreme Court rejects the idea of total incorporation; the idea of "fundamental" rights necessary to insure justice as opposed to "formal" rights; the "Honor Roll of Superior Rights"
7. the criminal law revolution; the 1960s as an era of major changes; the "Warren Court" incorporated almost all of the provisions of the Bill of Rights
8. *Griswold* v. *Connecticut* (1965); the U.S. Supreme Court recognizes a constitutionally protected right of personal privacy

G. Due process of law in the early 2000s
   1. current status of incorporation
   2. selective incorporation
   3. due process must be understood as asserting a fundamental principle of justice rather than a specific rule of law

H. Substantive due process
   1. concerns the content of the law; what the law says; is the law unreasonable or arbitrary in its subject matter?
   2. Void-for-Vagueness doctrine; laws found to be in violation of substantive due process because they were not clear about what behavior was prohibited
   3. *Buck* v. *Bell* (1927); the U.S. Supreme Court rules that a Virginia law allowing the sterilization of a mentally defective woman was not in violation of Fourteenth amendment due process
   4. *Skinner* v. *Oklahoma* (1942), U.S. Supreme Court rules sterilization unconstitutional

I. Procedural due process
   1. concerning the processes or procedures used by the government to carry out an action
   2. includes advance notice of proceedings, a hearing, opportunity to present a defense, impartial tribunal (fact finder), atmosphere of fairness

III. The Criminal Justice Process
   A. Prearrest investigation; examination of the scene of a crime, searching for evidence, interviewing witnesses, searching for the perpetrator; also, long-term investigations
   B. Arrest; taking a person into custody for the purpose of charging him/her with a crime
   C. Booking; police administrative procedures for recording an arrest
   D. Initial appearance; an arrestee's first appearance before a judge; formal notice of the charge
   E. Preliminary hearing; to protect defendants against unwarranted (unjustified) prosecutions
   F. Determination of formal charges
      1. indictment
      2. time bill
      3. no bill
      4. information
   G. Arraignment
      1. reading of formal charges
      2. defendant enters a plea, not guilty, guilty, nolo contendere, standing mute
   H. The trial process
      1. pretrial motions
      2. jury selection

3. the trial procedure
4. posttrial motions
- I. Sentencing (if found guilty); the imposition of punishment
- J. Appeals and release
  1. parole
  2. pardon
  3. reprieve
  4. commutation

IV. Criminal Justice as a "System"
   A. "System" indicates an orderly flow of managerial decision-making running from investigation to punishment
   B. The criminal justice "nonsystem"; a lack of unity of purpose among the police, courts, and corrections

V. Summary

REVIEW OF KEY TERMS, CONCEPTS, AND IDEAS

Write the definitions of the key terms in the space provided.

1. adversary system—

2. arrest—

3. *Barron v. Baltimore*—

4. Bill of Rights—

5. booking—

6. *Buck v. Bell*—

7. criminal justice process—

8. due process of law—

Chapter 5

9. *Gitlow* v. *New York*—_____
_____

10. *Griswold* v. *Connecticut*—_____
_____

11. inquiry system—_____
_____

12. inquisitorial system—_____
_____

13. procedural due process—_____
_____

14. rape shield statutes—_____
_____

15. substantive due process—_____
_____

16. void-for-vagueness doctrine—_____
_____

DISCUSSION

While the formal criminal justice process as described in Chapter 5 remains the predominant method of "doing justice" in the United States, in recent years alternative solutions to personal conflict have become increasingly popular. Much of the support for these alternatives to the criminal justice process has come from victims, rights advocates who argue that the traditional response to crime concentrates too much on the offender and not enough on the victim.

At least three criminal justice alternatives now provide crime victims with some means of effectively dealing with the people who have attacked them without having to rely on a criminal prosecution. These methods are mediation, civil lawsuits filed directly against the offender, and third-party lawsuits. Mediation is a process in which the victim and offender meet face-to-face and negotiate a settlement to the conflict. It is appropriate in cases where the victim is not especially interested in seeing the offender go to prison or receive some other criminal punishment. A big advantage of mediation for the victim is that it is usually much quicker, simpler, cheaper, and convenient than a formal criminal prosecution. Furthermore, since mediation is done in private, both the victim and the offender are able to avoid public scrutiny of their behavior before and during the crime. This is particularly important for victims whose conduct perhaps led up to or contributed to his/her victimization.

Finally, mediation can be effective in heading off future trouble between the parties to a dispute. While the criminal justice process is only concerned with past problems (the crime being prosecuted), mediation looks to the future and provides a means for some permanent solution to the conflict. This is important because many times unresolved disputes continue to escalate until one or both parties resort to violence to resolve the problem.

The second alternative to the criminal justice process, civil lawsuits against the perpetrator of the crime, were addressed in a recent publication of the Justice Department's Office for Victims of Crime ("Civil Legal Remedies for Crime Victims," 1993):

> Victims of crime are now resorting to civil litigation, in addition to victim compensation and restitution, as a financial means for recovering from the ill effects of crime. Increasingly, victims are finding their way into civil courtrooms to recover *from* physical, psychological and financial injuries by recovering *for* lost wages, hospital costs, counseling expenses, property damages and all of the many other various costs incurred as a result of victimization....
>
> In the criminal case, the prosecutor makes all decisions. He or she decides whether to file charges against an alleged perpetrator (*defendant*) based on an assessment of the legal adequacy of available evidence. Even though in some states the victim has a right to be consulted on plea agreements, it is largely within the prosecutor's discretion to decide whether to forgo a trial by accepting a plea on lesser charges in exchange for an admission of guilt. The prosecutor is responsible for *proving beyond a reasonable doubt* that an alleged perpetrator is guilty of the crimes charged (i.e., proving at least to a moral certainty). Failure to carry this burden of proof results in acquittal. A myriad of considerations, unrelated to the crime victim's victimization, may and often do affect the consequences faced by a perpetrator as a result of committing a crime.
>
> Civil litigation is important because it provides the victim with an opportunity to vindicate his or her individual rights and, in so doing, it provides empowerment. The victim decides whether or not to bring a civil suit. The victim decides whether to accept a settlement offer. It is up to the victim to carry the burden of proving liability by a *preponderance of the evidence* (i.e., proving by evidence which is more convincing than that presented by the other side). In a civil court, the victim controls essential decisions affecting the case against the perpetrator (the first party) and negligent third parties, parties who do not commit the crime but whose negligence may have facilitated the occurrence of the crime.

The last sentence in the above excerpt briefly introduces the final alternative to be discussed in this section, third-party lawsuits. The legal issues involved in third-party lawsuits are beyond the boundaries of this brief presentation, but the underlying factor concerns whether the action, inaction, or negligence of someone *other than* the perpetrator either caused the crime to occur or made it more likely that it could/would occur. Generally, the plaintiff (victim) must be able to prove by a preponderance of the evidence that the defendant had a duty or obligation to the plaintiff and that a breach (failure to uphold) of this obligation caused injury to the plaintiff. Examples of entities that have been successfully sued by crime victims include hotels, apartment complexes, universities, retail businesses, and police departments.

> Review the advantages (for the victim) of the alternatives to the criminal justice process addressed above, and list those advantages on one side of a sheet of paper. While the advantages seem to make these alternatives very tempting, one must also consider the disadvantages. Think about what some of these disadvantages may be and list those on the opposite side of your paper. Now, if you were a crime victim, would you prefer to rely on the traditional criminal justice process or one of the three alternatives?

38 Chapter 5

PRACTICE EXAM

The following practice exam will help you review the key terms, concepts, and ideas, discussed in this chapter. Score 2.5 points for each correct anwser.

MULTIPLE CHOICE

1. The inquisitorial system of justice was characterized by
    a. trial by ordeal.
    b. torture to obtain confessions.
    c. assumption of guilt.
    d. all of the above.

2. The first ten amendments to the U.S. Constitution are known as the
    a. guarantees of due process.
    b. due process rights.
    c. Bill of Rights.
    d. Preamble.

3. Which of the following was the major significance of the Bill of Rights?
    a. It placed restrictions on private citizens.
    b. It placed restrictions on business.
    c. It placed restrictions on government.
    d. It placed restrictions on private groups.

4. Substantive due process refers to
    a. the content of the law.
    b. the application of the law.
    c. the application of penalties.
    d. criminal procedure.

5. At issue in *Buck* v. *Bell* was (were)
    a. procedural due process.
    b. substantive due process.
    c. Fourth Amendment rights.
    d. probable cause.

6. Who of the following has the authority to issue an arrest warrant?
    a. any police officer
    b. any police officer other than the arresting officer
    c. the police captain
    d. a magistrate

7. _____ is the first point at which the accused may be released on bail.
   a. Preliminary hearing
   b. Arraignment
   c. Trial
   d. Booking

8. A plea is entered at the
   a. booking.
   b. initial appearance.
   c. preliminary hearing.
   d. arraignment.

9. The purpose of the preliminary hearing is to
   a. accept a plea.
   b. protect the accused from an unwarranted prosecution.
   c. initiate the *voir dire*.
   d. all of the above.

10. A judge may reject a guilty plea if
    a. he feels the defendant could not be convicted on the evidence of the prosecution.
    b. the defendant does not understand the consequences of the plea.
    c. the defendant is too poor to afford counsel.
    d. none of the above.

11. The accused may drop out of the criminal justice process at which of the following stages?
    a. the trial
    b. the initial appearance
    c. the preliminary hearing
    d. all of the above.

12. Which of the following is *not* true?
    a. The jury is "charged" by the judge.
    b. The vote of each individual juror is protected by a right of confidentiality.
    c. The jury is selected after the pretrial motions.
    d. None of the above.

13. _____ is a conditional release from prison.
    a. Probation
    b. Pardon
    c. Reprieve
    d. Parole

14. Due process of law refers to
    a. a system of trial by ordeal.
    b. fundamental principles of justice and the administration of laws that do not violate individual rights.
    c. the use of law by the court to uncover truth.
    d. inquisitorial justice.

15. The void-for-vagueness doctrine is an illustration of
    a. substantive due process.
    b. procedural due process.
    c. adversarial administration.
    d. the law of the land.

16. The first phase of the criminal justice process is generally the
    a. arrest.
    b. preliminary hearing.
    c. prearrest investigation.
    d. booking.

17. In criminal trials the _____ presents its case first.
    a. state
    b. court
    c. defense
    d. victim

18. *Griswold* v. *Connecticut* in 1965 dealt with
    a. freedom of religion.
    b. freedom of the press.
    c. double jeopardy.
    d. the right to privacy.

19. Which of the following provisions of the Bill of Rights has *not* as yet been incorporated?
    a. the Eighth Amendment protection against excessive fines
    b. the Fourth Amendment protection against illegal search and seizure
    c. the right to privacy
    d. the Eighth Amendment ban against cruel and unusual punishment

20. The author of the Bill of Rights was
    a. James Madison.
    b. Thomas Jefferson.
    c. Benjamin Franklin.
    d. John Hancock.

TRUE/FALSE

21. The inquisitorial system of justice was characterized by trial by ordeal, torture to obtain confessions, and the assumption of guilt.

22. Formal notice of the charge is given at the initial appearance.

23. A plea is entered at the preliminary hearing.

24. An information is filed by a prosecutor.

25. The grand jury's true bill will send the accused to trial.

26. A pardon is a "forgiveness" for the crime committed.

27. When a provision of the Bill of Rights is "incorporated," it is applicable to state and local government actions.

28. The "right to privacy" is not specifically cited in the Bill of Rights or anywhere else in the U.S. Constitution.

29. It was Supreme Court Justice Benjamin Cardozo who argued the distinction between "fundamental" rights and "formal" rights.

30. In *Barron* v. *Baltimore*, decided in 1833, the Supreme Court made it clear that the Bill of Rights provided no protection against state or local action, but only against that of federal authority.

FILL IN THE BLANK

31. Under the modern _____ system of justice, all persons are obliged to cooperate with the court in its quest for truth.

32. In the Fifth and _____ Amendments to the Constitution of the United States, we can find the "due process" clause.

33. During the Middle Ages, "due process" included _____ as a means of ascertaining guilt.

34. _____ is the act of taking a person into custody.

35. A _____ is a written order authorizing an arrest.

36. The _____ is a formal charging document based on a grand jury's determination whether there is sufficient indication to warrant a trial.

37. _____ is a conditional release from prison.

42 Chapter 5

38. A _____ is a "forgiveness" for the crime committed.

39. Under the issues of substantive due process and the _____ doctrine, statutes that are neither definite nor certain as to the categories of persons they refer to or the types of behavior that are forbidden are improper and unconstitutional.

40. The decision in *Powell* v. *Alabama* involved an indigent's right to _____ in capital cases.

ANSWERS TO THE PRACTICE EXAM

1. d
2. c
3. c
4. a
5. b
6. d
7. d
8. d
9. b
10. b
11. d
12. b
13. d
14. b
15. a
16. c
17. a
18. d
19. a
20. a
21. T
22. T
23. F
24. T
25. T
26. T
27. T
28. T
29. T
30. T
31. inquiry
32. Fourteenth
33. torture
34. Arrest
35. warrant
36. indictment
37. Parole
38. pardon
39. void-for-vagueness
40. counsel

CHAPTER 6

Police Systems in the United States: History and Structure

CHAPTER OUTLINE

I. Introduction

II. The Emergence of Modern Police; mutual pledge, sheriff, constable
   A. Magistrates, Constables, Beadles, and Thief-Takers
      1. nightwatch
      2. thief-takers or thief-makers?
      3. magistrates; judicial officials
      4. parish constables; limited powers of arrest
      5. beadles; constables, assistants
      6. thief-takers; private detectives who apprehended thieves and retrieved stolen property
   B. Henry Fielding and the Bow Street Runners
      1. foundation for the first modern police force
      2. Henry Fielding followed by his brother, John
      3. 1763; short-lived effort to operate a civilian Horse Patrol
      4. 1804; a second, more successful Horse Patrol set up as England's first uniformed police

44 Chapter 6

    C. Patrick Colquhoun and Sir Robert Peel
        1. resistance among the public toward a professional police force
        2. Colquhoun and the idea of a preventive police
        3. Peel and the London Metropolitan Police (1829)

II. Law and Order in Early America
    A. Colonial period
        1. the use of the military
        2. constables
        3. nightwatch
    B. The Trans-Mississippi West
        1. settlers moved faster than organized law enforcement and courts
        2. the sheriff as the primary police officer in the West
        3. posse comitatus; able-bodied men of the county who could be called on for assistance by the sheriff
        4. territorial agencies, the Texas Rangers
        5. federal marshals
    C. Policing the Metropolis
        1. 1845; the first metropolitan police force in the United States (New York City)
        2. responding to increased population, growing levels of poverty, and increase in crime
        3. by 1860, several other cities had NYC-style departments

III. Police Systems in the United States
    A. Thousands of independent police agencies representing all levels of government
        1. a single county may have several city police departments, sheriff's department, state police, federal agencies, private security, and special jurisdiction police
        2. jurisdiction; legal authority to enforce the law; geographic (within city, county, or state) and subject-matter (particular kinds of laws)
    B. Federal law enforcement agencies
        1. Department of Justice
            a. FBI
            b. DEA
            c. INS
            d. U.S. Marshals Service
            e. others
        2. Treasury Department
            a. Secret Service
            b. Bureau of Alcohol, Tobacco, and Firearms
            c. Customs Service
        3. U.S. Postal Service
        4. Department of Transportation—Coast Guard
        5. Department of Interior—National Park Service
        6. Inspectors General
        7. Other Federal Law Enforcement Agencies

Police Systems in the United States: History and Structure

    C. State police agencies
        1. Texas Rangers, Massachusetts State Constables
        2. weaknesses of the sheriff system; growth of state police agencies
        3. the beginning of modern state police administration
        4. 1905; Pennsylvania State Constabulary; first modern state police force
        5. two models
            a. general police powers
            b. highway patrol
    D. County and municipal policing
        1. policing is primarily done by county and municipal agencies
        2. sheriff or elected official
            a. law enforcement
            b. court service
        3. conflict between sheriffs and city police
    E. Police in the private sector
        1. historical antecedents (forerunners)
        2. significant growth in the United States in the past 100 years
        3. the Pinkertons
        4. private policing today
        5. problems with private policing
    F. Volunteer police and the vigilante tradition
        1. vigilante justice; individuals or groups take the law into their own hands to establish law and order
        2. present throughout the history of the United States
        3. modern groups such as the Guardian Angels
        4. auxiliary police groups that work with the local police; usually citizen volunteers

IV. Summary

REVIEW OF KEY TERMS, CONCEPTS, AND IDEAS

Write the definition of the key terms in the space provided.

1. Bow Street Runners—_____
   _____

2. Federal Bureau of Investigation—_____
   _____

3. Henry Fielding—_____
   _____

4. Interpol—_____
   _____

Chapter 6

5. mutual pledge—_____

6. *posse comitatus*—_____

7. Texas Rangers—_____

8. thief-takers—_____

9. vigilante justice—_____

DISCUSSION

I. The Texas Rangers

Take a virtual tour of the Texas Ranger Museum at http://www.texasranger.org/. The actual museum is located in Waco, Texas. Go to the Hall of Fame and read about some of the men who have served as Texas Rangers. Which Ranger tracked down and killed Bonnie and Clyde? Which one was born in Spain? How was Ranger Stanley Keith Guffey killed? Now go to Frequent Questions. What is the current authorized strength of the Texas Rangers? What are the qualifications to become a Texas Ranger? Who was the first African-American Texas Ranger in the modern era?

II. More About the State Police

Visit your state police Web site, and read about the history and organization of that department. What are the qualifications to become a trooper in your state? What is the starting salary and what benefits are provided?

III. Vigilante Justice

Historically, the police function was carried out by the citizens of a community. In the United States, vigilante groups were organized as early as the 1700s to fight lawlessness on the frontier. With the emergence of modern police forces in the early 1800s, the responsibility for keeping the peace and fighting crime shifted from a citizen-based model to a professional model. Review the section in the text which discusses vigilantes. Do you think that vigilantism can play a constructive role in today's society? Write a short essay stating your position on this issue.

IV. The Thin Blue Line

The police are often referred to as the "thin blue line," meaning that they are the only guardians of the peace, order, and safety of society. The implication is that if we did not have the police to protect us from the criminals, we would either quickly become a nation of victims or be forced to resort to individual violence to protect ourselves and our families. What do you think about this? Are the police really the "thin blue line" or is this just an image that the police have encouraged as a means of maintaining public support? Write a short essay in which you discuss your position.

PRACTICE EXAM

The following practice exam will help you review the key terms, concepts, and ideas discussed in this chapter. Give yourself 2.5 points for each correct answer. Answers are at the end of the exam.

MULTIPLE CHOICE

1. Structurally, law enforcement in the United States has the characteristic of
   a. centralization.
   b. decentralization.
   c. interdependency.
   d. nationalization.

2. Under the mutual pledge system of policing _____, were ten families grouped together who had responsibility for the acts of their members.
   a. hundreds
   b. shires
   c. sheriffs
   d. tithings

3. _____ can be credited with laying the foundation for the first modern police force.
   a. Sir Robert Peel
   b. Henry Fielding
   c. John Fielding
   d. Patrick Colquhoun

4. The first organized force ever used in England against criminals was known as
   a. the Bow Street Runners.
   b. the Hyde Park Police.
   c. the "Peelers."
   d. the London Bobbies.

5. West of the Mississippi, the first formal law enforcement agents to appear were
   a. sheriffs.
   b. town marshals.
   c. federal marshals.
   d. the Texas Rangers.

6. The *posse comitatus*
   a. consisted of all the able-bodied men in a county.
   b. was organized as a corps to protect the settlers from the Indians.
   c. was the name given to juries in barroom justice.
   d. was a confederation of private police agencies.

7. The Bow Street Runners
    a. were the creation of Henry Fielding.
    b. were paid as thief-takers.
    c. laid the foundation for the modern police.
    d. all of the above.

8. The Texas Rangers
    a. were the first state police body in America.
    b. were a fighting force in the Texas Revolution.
    c. were created to protect settlers from Indians.
    d. all of the above.

9. The first metropolitan police force in Europe appeared in
    a. Paris.
    b. Rome.
    c. London.
    d. Brussels.

10. The Border Patrol is a part of the
    a. Immigration and Naturalization Service.
    b. Bureau of Alcohol, Tobacco and Firearms.
    c. Customs Service.
    d. U.S. Marshal Service.

11. Interpol functions as
    a. an investigative body.
    b. a data depository.
    c. an enforcement body.
    d. a division of the Department of Justice.

12. State police agencies emerged in response to
    a. federal efforts to create a national police force.
    b. the inability of the U.S. courts to enforce their powers.
    c. the weaknesses in the sheriff system and the more global nature of crime.
    d. the unwillingness of the federal agencies to patrol state lands.

13. Which of the following represents the most critical problem for private police agencies?
    a. the strict controls placed on them by state legislatures
    b. the high cost of salaries and equipment
    c. the strict limits placed on their authority
    d. the inadequate training of their employees

14. The vigilante tradition refers to
    a. the neighborhood watch groups in urban communities.
    b. the organized and extralegal movements of persons who take the law into their own hands.
    c. the frontier lynch mobs who disagreed with courtroom justice.
    d. any of the above.

15. Auxiliary police reserves
    a. are uniformed, paid civilians under the supervision of local police.
    b. are armed and uniformed groups with powers similar to those of full-time officers.
    c. are unarmed but have formal enforcement powers.
    d. do not have the power to arrest.

16. Congress opposed the creation of the FBI because
    a. it seemed too expensive.
    b. there were already too many law enforcement agencies at the federal level.
    c. it feared that a "secret police" would be created.
    d. all of the above.

17. Modern police agencies in the U.S.
    a. have fixed, exclusive jurisdictions.
    b. frequently have overlapping jurisdictions, often leading to disputes between agencies.
    c. are coordinated by the federal government.
    d. all have the same level of authority to enforce the law.

18. The majority of law enforcement and peacekeeping activity is provided by
    a. sheriffs.
    b. federal agencies.
    c. state police agencies.
    d. county and municipal authority.

19. The _____ is a joint federal, state and local law enforcement initiative against high-level drug trafficking organizations.
    a. FBI-FEA-ATF coalition
    b. South Florida Crack Task Force
    c. Organized Crime Drug Enforcement Task Force Program
    d. High Intensity Anti-Crime Unit

20. The high crime rates in Rio de Janeiro, Brazil, have been attributed to
    a. a high index of poverty.
    b. a lack of funding for law enforcement activities.
    c. escalating levels of drug use and trafficking.
    d. choices a and c above.
    e. none of the above.

TRUE/FALSE

21. The English were opposed to a professional police force because of their belief that police were instruments of oppression.

22. The first metropolitan police force in the United States appeared in Philadelphia.

23. The Border Patrol is part of the Immigration and Naturalization Service.

24. In the years following the Civil War and Reconstruction, the office of the sheriff emerged as the most effective form of rural law enforcement.

25. The FBI was organized because the Justice Department had no detectives of its own.

26. The U.S. Marshal Service is the chief investigative body of the Department of Justice.

27. In recent years municipalities have turned to private organizations for the provision of services typically performed by public police and sheriff's departments.

28. The term "private eye" comes from the logo of the Pinkerton Detective Agency.

29. Federal marshals were established by the Constitution of the United States.

30. Civilian auxiliary units in urban police departments have full enforcement powers and are authorized to carry weapons.

FILL IN THE BLANK

31. Policing emerged during the rule of England's _____.

32. The _____ system organized the community into tithings, hundreds, and shires.

33. The investigative units of the _____ focus on the forgery and counterfeiting of U.S. currency, checks, bonds, and federal food stamps.

34. In addition to the FBI, the _____ has legal jurisdiction extending to all federal crimes that are not the specific responsibility of some other federal law enforcement agency.

35. The best known and perhaps the most controversial of today's vigilante associations is the _____.

36. In contrast to vigilantes _____, police groups consist of civilians working with local police.

37. Violations of the Civil Rights Act fall under the jurisdiction of the _____.

38. A _____ was a group of able-bodied men of a county who were at the disposal of a sheriff for service.

39. _____ is an international police organization that serves as a depository of intelligence information on wanted criminals.

40. The _____ is the U.S. representative to Interpol.

ANSWERS TO THE PRACTICE EXAM

1. b	15. a	29. F
2. d	16. c	30. F
3. b	17. b	31. Alfred the Great
4. a	18. d	32. mutual pledge
5. a	19. c	33. Secret Service
6. a	20. d	34. U.S. Marshal Service
7. d	21. T	35. Guardian Angels
8. d	22. F	36. auxiliary
9. c	23. T	37. FBI
10. a	24. F	38. *posse comitatus*
11. b	25. F	39. Interpol
12. c	26. F	40. Treasury Department
13. d	27. T	
14. b	28. T	

CHAPTER 7

Enforcing the Law and Keeping the Peace: The Nature and Scope of Police Work

CHAPTER OUTLINE

I. The Functions of Police
   A. The role of police
      1. most police work involves peacekeeping as opposed to crime fighting (law enforcing)
      2. crime prevention and protection of the public; the importance of patrol
      3. additional tasks usually conducted out of public view
      4. about 20 percent of arrests each year are for Index crimes
      5. peacekeeping activities as precriminal activity
   B. The right to use force
      1. peacekeeping role, the legitimate right to use force in situations whose urgency requires it
      2. the right to use force in modern democratic society has been taken away from the citizen and given to the police.

II. The Police Bureaucracy
   A. Police organized around the military model
   B. Division of labor, assignment of similar types of work to particular units (training, patrol, juvenile division, investigations, etc.), allows persons to do the same type of work on a regular basis

C. Chain and units of command
   1. information flow up and down the organization
   2. each person knows to whom he/she is accountable
   3. use of military-style rank structure (captains, lieutenants, sergeants, etc.)
D. Rules, regulation, and discipline
   1. handbooks, manuals, and other written rules covering conduct, administrative procedures, arrest, etc.
   2. conflict between proper conduct and making a lawful arrest
   3. no rules can cover all possible situations
E. Problems of enforcement
F. Strategic leniency
   1. supervisors ignore many minor violations
   2. quasi-military punitive approach to rule enforcement
   3. military model may be inappropriate for policing

III. The Organization of Policing
   A. Administrative components
      1. line services, patrol, investigation, traffic
      2. administrative services, training, planning, legal matters, etc., to support the line services
      3. auxiliary services, communications, record keeping, laboratory, etc., to assist the line services in performing the basic police functions
   B. Patrol, the backbone of policing
      1. variety of tasks
      2. functions of police patrol
         a. protect public safety
         b. enforce the law
         c. control traffic
         d. conduct criminal investigations
         e. quasi-judicial functions
      3. motorized versus foot patrols
      4. Kansas City Preventive Patrol Experiment
   C. Detective work
      1. duties and responsibilities
         a. identification, location, and apprehension of offenders
         b. collection and preservation of evidence
         c. location and interviewing of witnesses
         d. recovery and return of stolen property
      2. duties and organization vary by size of department-specialized investigative units
      3. effectiveness
      4. evaluation of detectives, clearance rates
   D. Specialized police units
      1. juvenile division or youth bureau
      2. decoys and blending
      3. web patrols
      4. SWAT
      5. sting operations

IV. Community Policing
   A. community responsiveness
   B. assignment of officers to a specific neighborhood
   C. importance of communication with residents of the community
   D. broken windows
   E. obstacles to community policing

V. Women in Policing
   A. The emergence of women police
      1. early history
      2. Alice Stubbins Wells and the L.A.P.D.
   B. The equal opportunity movement for women in policing
      1. Civil Rights Act of 1964
      2. EEOA of 1972
      3. Title VII of the Civil Rights Act
      4. *Griggs* v. *Duke Power Co.*
      5. *Blake* v. *Los Angeles*
   C. Current status of women in policing
      1. research supports women's ability to do police work well
      2. continuing problems of harassment and bias

VI. Police Discretion and Selective Law Enforcement
   A. Police officers as law interpreters
   B. Importance of police discretion, department and individual officer
   C. Selective enforcement of the law
   D. Situations requiring discretion
      1. questionable legislative intent
      2. limited police resources
      3. situational determinants
   E. Full enforcement of the law, impossible and undesirable
   F. Factors in the decision to arrest
      1. seriousness of the offense
      2. weapons involvement
      3. desires of complainant/witness
      4. attitude and character of offender
   G. Command discretion
      1. departmental objectives
      2. enforcement policies
      3. deployment of resources

VII. The Police Subculture
   A. Subculture as a smaller group within a larger group with different beliefs, values, and attitudes; the police subculture

Chapter 7

    B. The police personality
        1. danger and authority; working personality
        2. police cynicism
    C. Sources of stress

VIII. Summary

REVIEW OF KEY TERMS, CONCEPTS, AND IDEAS

Write the definitions of the key terms in the space provided.

1. clearance rate—

2. community policing—

3. full enforcement—

4. patrol—

5. peacekeeping role—

6. police cynicism—

7. police discretion—

8. police subculture—

9. working personality—

DISCUSSION

Read the following scenario and write a one page essay explaining what you would do in this situation and giving your reasons for choosing this particular course of action.

You are a probationary police officer and this is the first week that you have patrolled on your own without a partner or Field Training Officer; you have been with the department for about 3 months. Your town has a population of about 50,000 people. You were born here, graduated from high school here, and attended the local college majoring in criminal justice. You know the town well and have many friends in the community. This is a nice place to live and work, and you hope that you can make a career here, settle down, start a family, maybe even be Chief of Police someday.

One night while on patrol, you spot a car driving at an excessive speed down a street in a residential neighborhood. You begin a pursuit and notice that the car weaves across the center line several times. You finally pull the car over thinking that this is a drunk driver who is obviously a danger to the community. When you approach the car, you see that the driver is your old friend from high school, Jerry. Jerry seems intoxicated, but he recognizes you and gives you a friendly greeting. After a few minutes of small talk, during which you smell a strong alcohol odor on Jerry, you tell him that you want him to perform a field sobriety test. He looks at you with surprise and says, "You're kidding, right?"

You reply, "No Jerry, I'm not kidding. I think you're drunk, and you shouldn't be driving. I may have to arrest you."

"Aw man," says Jerry, "you wouldn't do that to your old bud, would you?"

Jerry fails the field sobriety test badly. "Yes, I'm afraid so" you respond. "Get in the back seat."

"Wait a minute," says Jerry, "maybe I had a little too much, but I'm on my way home—you know where I live—it's just a couple of blocks. Man, I don't need this. My insurance is already sky high; if I get a DWI, it will go out of sight! You gotta cut me some slack!"

"Sorry Jerry, but this is serious. You could hurt someone, or kill someone, even yourself. Let's go."

"Come on," Jerry pleads, "I know it's serious, but I need a break. Besides, I didn't turn you in that night I got busted smoking grass in high school."

Suddenly, you flash back. It was the summer after 10th grade and you and a bunch of your friends were at the park. Someone brought out some marijuana and started passing it around. It was only minutes until a sheriff's deputy drove up and everyone scattered. Jerry was the only one who got caught; he ended up on juvenile probation, but never told anyone else who was there that night. You feel both stupid and afraid. Jerry's right—he did cover for you. You were a kid then, and it was really no big deal, but this is different—you're a cop now, and this is your job. But, what if Jerry tells the Chief about the marijuana incident? What about your credibility as a police officer if this becomes public knowledge? It's not so much about the marijuana now as it is about your honesty. When you filled out your job application, you answered "no" to the question about any prior drug use.

What do you do?

PRACTICE EXAM

The following practice exam will help you review the key terms, concepts, and ideas discussed in this chapter. Give yourself 2.5 points for each correct answer. Answers are at the end of the exam.

MULTIPLE CHOICE

1. Most police work involves
   a. enforcing the law.
   b. apprehending criminals.
   c. keeping the peace.
   d. directing traffic.

2. Police organizations are structured along a _____ model.
   a. line service
   b. departmental
   c. linear
   d. bureaucratic

3. Which of the following is an incorrect statement regarding police?
   a. Police procedures are explicit and comprehensive regarding how to handle various domestic situations.
   b. Observers of police activity agree that many police rules and regulations are essentially useless and are for the most part unenforcable.
   c. The police process demands compliance with departmental regulations as well as vigorous law enforcement, and these demands are sometimes in conflict.
   d. What the officer must do depends more often on the nuances of the situation than on any regulation or published procedure.

4. Which of the following is true about police regulations?
   a. They are often sacrificed to make a "good" arrest.
   b. They are generally impossible to enforce.
   c. They are often too vague to cover actual street situations.
   d. All of the above.

5. The most visible and primary parts of policing are
   a. the line services.
   b. the staff services.
   c. the auxiliary services.
   d. the special services.

6. Police administrative services include
   a. patrol and domestic intervention.
   b. legal matters.
   c. data processing and payroll.
   d. internal investigations.

7. _____ is the most basic aspect of police work.
   a. Patrol
   b. Order maintenance
   c. Adherence to regulations
   d. Discretion

8. In a study conducted by the Police Foundation in 1972–73, three different levels of preventive patrol in Kansas City were closely compared. "Normal" patrols involved a single car cruising the streets when not responding to calls; "proactive" patrols involved doubling or tripling the number of cruising cars; "reactive" patrols involved eliminating police cruisers altogether, with police entering the areas designated for study only in response to specific requests. The results of the Kansas City experiment showed that
   a. "proactive" patrols were most effective in reducing crime.
   b. "normal" patrols were most effective in reducing crime.
   c. "proactive" and "normal" patrols were equally effective, yet crime increased where "reactive" patrols were used.
   d. there were no differences in effectiveness regardless of the kind of patrol.

9. Which of the following is most true of detectives?
   a. They investigate almost all serious crimes and make a proportionately large number arrests.
   b. They investigate almost all serious crimes and make proportionately few arrests.
   c. They investigate only a few select serious crimes and make arrests for most of them.
   d. They investigate only a few serious crimes and make few arrests.

10. A crime is considered "cleared" when
    a. a detective is assigned to investigate it.
    b. a detective completes an investigation.
    c. an arrest is made.
    d. the suspect has been convicted.

11. "Multiple clearance" occurs when
    a. a conspiracy arrest occurs.
    b. two or more individuals are arrested for a single crime.
    c. the arrest of one person results in the clearing of numerous other crimes.
    d. one member of a gang is arrested for an act performed by the entire gang.

12. _____ is a formal declaration that certain crimes previously thought to have occurred never actually happened.
    a. Reclassification
    b. Reduction
    c. Defounding
    d. Unfounding

13. Blending includes
    a. patrol and detective units working together to solve special cases.
    b. police posing as ordinary citizens to observe and intervene if a crime occurs.
    c. the socialization of police officers into the police subculture.
    d. all of the above.

14. In _____ operations, nonuniformed police officers pose as high risk victims.
    a. blending
    b. decoy
    c. entrapment
    d. tactical patrol

15. "Sting" operations involve the use of various undercover methods to
    a. identify corrupt politicians.
    b. apprehend drug traffickers.
    c. entrap dishonest police officers.
    d. control large-scale theft.

16. Police discretion exists
    a. only in large urban departments with complex bureaucratic structures.
    b. primarily in rural sheriffs, departments where supervision of officers in the field is impossible.
    c. whenever an officer or police agency is free to choose among various alternatives.
    d. particularly in those circumstances where the facts of the situation are so clear-cut that only one course of action is possible.

17. A police officer may decide not to arrest when
    a. the offense is trivial.
    b. the victim is a party to the offense.
    c. an arrest would cause undue harm to the offender.
    d. all of the above.

18. A subculture is
    a. an organization or group of individuals that represents only a small part of the dominant culture.
    b. a body of rules descriptive of the norms of the wider society.
    c. the normative system of a particular group that is smaller than and essentially different from the dominant culture.
    d. the style of life of a group newly assimilated into a larger society.

19. The two elements of the police role that serve to shape the "working personality" of police are
    a. boredom and routine.
    b. militarism and conservatism.
    c. suspicion and fear.
    d. danger and authority.

20. Recent studies suggest that the cynicism and authoritarianism manifested by many police officers are due to
    a. the type of persons policing attracts.
    b. the nature of police socialization.
    c. the lack of a uniform command structure.
    d. the lack of police professionalization.

21. _____ refers to the notion that all people are motivated by evil and selfishness.
    a. Police ambivalence
    b. Police paranoia
    c. Police cynicism
    d. Police solidarity

22. The greatest number of assaults on police officers occur while they are
    a. investigating felonies.
    b. arresting felony criminals.
    c. responding to "disturbance calls."
    d. engaging in riot and crowd control.

23. The police role is separate from that of the private citizen because the police
    a. cannot file civil suits.
    b. have the legitimate right to use force.
    c. spend most of their time making arrests for Index crimes.
    d. are members of a bureaucratic organization.

24. The _____ components of police organizations provide support for the _____ services of policing, which include such activities as patrol and investigation.
    a. administrative, line
    b. line, auxiliary
    c. auxiliary, internal
    d. investigative, line

25. The first interpretation of whether a law has been violated is
    a. a matter for which there are strict procedures to follow and little discretion.
    b. usually made by patrol officers.
    c. the job of detectives in the investigative division.
    d. made by the patrol officer's supervisor in most cases.

TRUE/FALSE

26. People's negative opinions about police work and behavior come mainly from a lack of understanding of the nature of police work.

27. FBI data suggest that the largest proportion of police arrest activity relates to such crimes as burglary, larceny, and other thefts.

62 Chapter 7

28. For more than a century, the "cop on the beat" was the very symbol of policing in America. Beginning with the 1930s, however, police foot patrols began to disappear. Today, these patrols have been fully replaced by highly mobile forces of one- and two-person cars.

29. Detectives more typically focus their energies on assault and rape cases, as opposed to burglary and theft cases, because the victims can more often provide clues that make the cases easier to solve.

30. Police discretion exists only in large urban departments with complex bureaucratic structures.

31. The phrase "rule of thumb" refers to the police practice of examining a wife's bruises from her husband's beating; if her bruises were larger than the width of a thumb, her husband was taken into custody and charged with spousal abuse.

32. Police officers often use discretion when a law is vague and/or ambiguous.

33. The peacekeeping role of the police involves the legitimate right to use force in situations in which urgency requires it.

34. Patrol is the primary activity of detectives.

35. Detectives "clear" far fewer cases than larger number of officers assigned to patrol duties.

FILL IN THE BLANK

36. The largest operating unit of a police force is _____.

37. A crime is considered "cleared" when _____.

38. Virtually every police organization in the Western world is structured around a _____ model.

39. At the apex of the police peacekeeping role is the legitimate right to _____ in situations which demand it.

40. The restriction on a citizen's right to use force settling disputes extends to all matters except _____.

ANSWERS TO THE PRACTICE EXAM

1. c
2. d
3. a
4. d
5. a
6. b
7. a
8. d
9. b
10. c
11. c
12. d
13. b
14. b
15. d
16. c
17. d
18. c
19. d
20. b
21. c
22. c
23. b
24. a
25. b
26. T
27. F
28. F
29. T
30. F
31. F
32. T
33. T
34. F
35. T
36. patrol
37. an arrest is made
38. military
39. use force
40. self-defense

CHAPTER 8

The Law of Arrest, Search, and Seizure: Police and the Constitution

CHAPTER OUTLINE

I. Search and Seizure, The Fourth Amendment
  A. Search, the examination or inspection of premises or person with a view to discovering stolen or illicit (unlawful) property or evidence of guilt, investigation and evidence gathering
  B. "Unreasonable" as an ambiguous term
  C. Search warrant, a written order, issued by a magistrate (judge) and directed to a law enforcement officer, commanding a search of a specified premises
  D. Probable cause; *Illinois v. Gates*

II. Warrantless Search
  A. Search incident to arrest
    1. in order for the search to be lawful, the arrest must be lawful
    2. limitation on scope—*Chimel v. California*
    3. consequences of unlawful arrest
  B. Stop and frisk (field interrogation)
    1. useful tool for police, especially in high crime areas
    2. *Terry* v. *Ohio* (1968), police officer who stops a suspicious person may frisk (pat down) the person's outer clothing as a check for a weapon

66 Chapter 8

        3. fruit of the poisonous tree, evidence seized illegally is "tainted" and cannot be used against a suspect
        4. *Minnesota* v. *Dickerson* (1993), the "plain feel" doctrine as an expansion of stop and frisk
   C. Automobile Searches
        1. Carroll doctrine (1925), allowing warrantless searches of automobiles
        2. Police spot checks, for checking driver's licenses and vehicle registrations, in *Delaware* v. *Prouse* (1979)
        3. *Indianapolis v. Edmond*
   D. Fresh Pursuit
        1. following a fleeing suspect who is endeavoring to avoid immediate capture
        2. the danger of higher speed automobile chases
   E. Consent searches
        1. requires neither probable cause nor a search warrant
        2. consent must be given must freely and knowingly
        3. *Florida* v. *Bostick* (1991)
   F. Other warrantless searches
        1. searches by private individuals
        2. border searches
        3. inventory searches
        4. electronic eavesdropping
        5. abandoned property
        6. expectation of privacy (garbage searches)
        7. open fields

III. The "Plain View" Doctrine
   A. *Harris* v. *United States* (1968)
   B. Anything that a police officer sees in plain view, when that officer has a right to be where he or she is, is not the product of a search and is therefore admissible as evidence
   C. Protective sweeps doctrine

IV. The Exclusionary Rule
   A. Prohibition against the use, in court, of illegally obtained evidence
   B. *Weeks* v. *United States* (1914), U.S. Supreme Court initiates the exclusionary rule to apply in federal court
   C. "Silver platter" doctrine, evidence seized through unreasonable search and seizure by state agents could be turned over to federal agents and used in court
   D. *Wolf* v. *Colorado* (1949), the Fourth Amendment protects individuals against state as well as federal action, but the exclusionary rule does not apply in state courts
   E. *Rochin* v. *California* (1952), evidence obtained in violation of the Fourth Amendment must be excluded from use in state as well as federal trials
   F. *Mapp* v. *Ohio* (1961), U.S. Supreme Court extends the exclusionary rule to state courts
   G. The impact of *Mapp*
   H. The retreat from *Mapp*
        1. *United States* v. *Calandra* (1974)
        2. the "good faith" exception to the exclusionary rule (*United States* v. *Leon*, 1984)

V. Custodial Interrogation
   A. The Fifth and Sixth Amendments
   B. *Twining* v. *New Jersey* (1908) state defendants not protected by Fifth Amendment
   C. *Brown* v. *Mississippi* (1936), confessions obtained by physical coercion cannot be used in state court
   D. The prompt arraignment rule, McNabb and Mallory cases
   E. Confessions and counsel
      1. Sixth Amendment right to counsel (attorney)
      2. *Escobedo* v. *Illinois* (1964), U.S. Supreme Court rules that the accused must be permitted to have his or her attorney present during interrogation
   F. *Miranda* v. *Arizona* (1966)
      1. produced the *Miranda* warning
      2. controversy over the impact of the ruling or ability of police to fight crime
   G. Show-ups, lineups, and exemplars
      1. show-up, one-on-one presentation of a suspect to a victim
      2. lineup, victim is asked to pick a suspect from a group of persons
      3. *United States* v. *Wade* (1967) suspect has a right to his or her attorney during a lineup
   H. DNA and other nontestimonial exemplars
      1. DNA and forensic science
      2. blood, voice, handwriting

VI. Summary

REVIEW OF KEY TERMS, IDEAS, AND CONCEPTS

Write the definitions of the key terms in the space provided.

1. Carroll doctrine—_____

2. *Chimel* v. *California*—_____

3. *Delaware* v. *Prouse*—_____

4. *Escobedo* v. *Illinois*—_____

5. exclusionary rule—_____

6. *Florida* v. *Bostick*—_____

7. fruit of the poisonous tree—

8. *Illinois* v. *Gates*—

9. *Illinois v. Wardlow*—

10. *Indianapolis v. Edmond*—

11. *Mapp* v. *Ohio*—

12. *Minnesota* v. *Dickerson*—

13. *Miranda* v. *Arizona*—

14. "plain view" doctrine—

15. probable cause—

16. protective sweep doctrine—

17. *Rochin* v. *California*—

18. search and seizure—

19. search warrant—

20. *Terry* v. *Ohio*—

21. *United States* v. *Leon*—

22. *United States* v. *Wade*—_____
_____

23. *Weeks* v. *United States*—_____
_____

DISCUSSION

One of the early U.S. Supreme Court cases concerning search and seizure is known as *Katz* v. *United States*. A portion of the Court's opinion in this case is given below. Also included is a portion of Justice Harlan's concurring opinion. Read this material carefully and then go on to the questions that follow.

KATZ v. UNITED STATES

389 U.S. 347, 88 S.Ct. 507, 19 L.Ed.2d 576 (1967)

MR. JUSTICE STEWART delivered the opinion of the Court.

The petitioner was convicted in the District Court for the Southern District of California under an eight-count indictment charging him with transmitting wagering information by telephone from Los Angeles to Miami and Boston, in violation of a federal statute. At trial the Government was permitted, over the petitioner's objection, to introduce evidence of the petitioner's end of telephone conversations, overheard by FBI agents who had attached an electronic listening and recording device to the outside of the public telephone booth from which he had placed his calls. In affirming his conviction, the Court of Appeals rejected the contention that the recordings had been obtained in violation of the Fourth Amendment because "{t}here was no physical entrance into the area occupied by {the petitioner}." We granted certiorari in order to consider the constitutional questions thus presented.

The petitioner has phrased those questions as follows:

"A. Whether a public telephone booth is a constitutionally protected area so that evidence obtained by attaching an electronic listening recording device to the top of such a booth is obtained in violation of the right to privacy of the user of the booth.

"B. Whether physical penetration of a constitutionally protected area is necessary before a search and seizure can be said to be violative of the Fourth Amendment to the United States Constitution."

We decline to adopt this formulation of the issues. In the first place, the correct solution of Fourth Amendment problems is not necessarily promoted by incantation of the phrase "constitutionally protected area." Secondly, the Fourth Amendment cannot be translated into a general constitutional "right to privacy." That Amendment protects individual privacy against certain kinds of governmental intrusion, but its protections go further, and often have nothing to do with privacy at all . . . .

Because of the misleading way the issues have been formulated, the parties have attached great significance to the characterization of the telephone booth from which petitioner placed his calls. The petitioner has strenuously argued that the booth was a "constitutionally protected area." The Government has maintained with equal vigor that it was not. But this effort to decide whether or not a given "area," viewed in the abstract, is "constitutionally protected" deflects attention from the problem presented by this case. For the Fourth Amendment protects people, not places. What a person knowingly exposes to the public, even in his own home or office, is not a subject of Fourth Amendment protection . . . . But what he seeks to preserve as private, even in an area accessible to the public, may be constitutionally protected . . . .

No less than an individual in a business office, in a friend's apartment, or in a taxicab, a person in a telephone booth may rely upon the protection of the Fourth Amendment. One who occupies it, shuts the door behind him, and pays the toll that permits him to place a call is surely entitled to assume that the words he utters into the mouthpiece will not be broadcast to the world . . . .

The Government's activities in electronically listening to and recording the petitioner's words violated the privacy upon which he justifiably relied while using the telephone booth and thus constituted a "search and seizure" within the meaning of the Fourth Amendment. The fact that the electronic device employed to achieve that end did not happen to penetrate the wall of the booth can have no constitutional significance . . . .

Wherever a man may be, he is entitled to know that he will remain free from unreasonable searches and seizures . . . . the judgement must be reversed.

It is so ordered.

MR. JUSTICE HARLAN, concurring.

I join the opinion of the Court. . . .

As the Court's opinion states, "the Fourth Amendment protects people, not places." The question, however, is what protection it affords to those people. Generally, as here, the answer to that question requires reference to a "place." My understanding of the rule that has emerged from prior decisions is that there is a twofold requirement, first that a person have exhibited an actual (subjective) expectation of privacy and, second, that the expectation be one that society is prepared to recognize as "reasonable." Thus a man's home is, for most purposes, a place where he expects privacy, but objects, activities, or statements that he exposes to the "plain view" of outsiders are not "protected" because no intention to keep them to himself has been exhibited.

QUESTIONS

1. Imagine that Mr. Katz had placed his telephone calls from the following locations. Could the Supreme Court's ruling have been different in any of these situations?
    A. a telephone mounted on the wall of a corridor at a busy airport
    B. a telephone sitting on the bar at a local tavern
    C. a telephone booth which was designed and built without a door

2. How would the "reasonable expectation of privacy" referred to by Justice Harlan be evaluated in each of the situations given in Question 1? Is "reasonable expectation of privacy" something that a person either has or does not have in some absolute form, or does it exist "more or less," depending on the situation?

3. What is the significance of the Supreme Court's statement that the "Fourth Amendment protects people, not places"? Why was this idea an important part of this case?

PRACTICE EXAM

The following practice exam will help you reviews the key terms, concepts and ideas discussed in this chapter. Give yourself 2.5 points for each correct answer. Answers are at the end of the exam.

MULTIPLE CHOICE

1. The Fourth Amendment protects citizens from
   a. police use of deadly force.
   b. double jeopardy.
   c. cruel and unusual punishment.
   d. unreasonable search and seizure.

2. "Unreasonable" searches and seizures, in constitutional terms, are those that are
   a. conducted without a warrant.
   b. crudely and rudely done.
   c. not justified by the apparent facts.
   d. undertaken in the absence of the accused's attorney.

3. _____ refers to facts or apparent facts that are reliable and generate a reasonable belief that a crime has been committed.
   a. Evidence-in-chief
   b. Probable cause
   c. *Factum a judice quod*
   d. *Priori pentente*

4. The issue in *Terry* v. *Ohio* was the legal status of
   a. resisting an unlawful arrest.
   b. no-knock statutes.
   c. consent searches.
   d. stop and frisk procedures.

5. *Harris* v. *United States* established the
   a. exclusionary rule.
   b. "plain view" doctrine.
   c. protective sweep doctrine.
   d. Carroll doctrine.

6. According to the "plain view" doctrine,
    a. anything a police officer sees, even though it may be in his "plain view," cannot be automatically seized.
    b. evidence in "plain view" that is seized by an officer represents the product of a search and is thus subject to Fourth Amendment restrictions.
    c. evidence (1) in the immediate vicinity of a suspect already in custody and (2) in "plain view" of the officer is subject to warrantless seizure.
    d. whatever a police officer happens to see in plain view when he has a right to be where he is, is not the subject of a search and is therefore admissible as evidence.

7. A full search of a suspect is permitted in
    a. a felony arrest.
    b. a misdemeanor arrest.
    c. a traffic arrest.
    d. a and b above.
    e. all of the above.

8. *Wolf* v. *Colorado* dealt with
    a. illegal search and seizure.
    b. prompt arraignment.
    c. no-knock statutes.
    d. show-ups and line-ups.
    e. illegal confessions.

9. *Coolidge* v. *New Hampshire* involved issues in
    a. arrest.
    b. probable cause seizure.
    c. arrest-search.
    d. plain-view seizure.
    e. all of the above

10. The retreat from *Mapp* began with
    a. *United States* v. *Calandra*.
    b. *Escobedo* v. *Illinois*.
    c. *Wolf* v. *Colorado*.
    d. *United States* v. *Janis*.
    e. *Stone* v. *Powell*.

11. Involuntary confessions are prohibited by the _____ Amendment.
    a. Fourth
    b. Fifth
    c. Sixth
    d. Eighth

12. The assistance of counsel is guaranteed by the _____ Amendment.
    a. Fourth
    b. Fifth and Fourteenth
    c. Sixth
    d. Eighth

13. The *McNabb-Mallory* rule refers to
    a. state agents supplying federal prosecutors with evidence obtained in violation of the Fourth Amendment.
    b. the authority of police to search entire premises if they make an arrest on the premises.
    c. evidence gathered during delay in arraigning a suspect.
    d. evidence obtained through the use of physical coercion.

14. The *McNabb-Mallory* prompt arraignment rule was modified by
    a. *Brown* v. *Mississippi*.
    b. the Omnibus Crime Control and Safe Streets Act.
    c. *Brewer* v. *Williams*.
    d. It was never modified.

15. The "right to remain silent" is part of the
    a. Carroll doctrine.
    b. prompt arraignment rule.
    c. *Miranda* warning rules.
    d. no-knock statutes.

16. The Supreme Court's "retreat from *Miranda*" occurred under the leadership of
    a. Richard Nixon.
    b. Earl Warren.
    c. Warren Burger.
    d. the Senate Judiciary Committee.

17. The "Christian burial speech" in the case of _____ was found to be in violation of the Fifth Amendment.
    a. *Brewer* v. *Williams*
    b. *Mapp* v. *Ohio*
    c. *Wolf* v. *Colorado*
    d. *Miranda* v. *Arizona*
    e. *Harris* v. *New York*

18. Police powers are generally divided into two major categories; these are referred to as _____ and _____ powers.
    a. frisk, search
    b. investigative, arrest
    c. search, seizure
    d. administrative, line

TRUE/FALSE

19. The common law rule of arrest permits a police officer to make an arrest without a warrant in any felony case.

20. The common law of "fresh pursuit" relates to the following of a fleeing suspect who is endeavoring to avoid immediate capture, and has been adopted by most state jurisdictions.

21. Warrantless searches may be undertaken by law enforcement officers when the person in control of the area or object consents to a search. However, in the opinion of the U.S. Supreme Court, all consents to search are "limited" consents.

22. The issue in *Rochin* v. *California* involved evidence acquired in a manner that "shocks the conscience."

23. The significance of *Chimel* v. *California* was that it expanded police officers' authority to search for destructible evidence.

24. Russian president Boris Yeltsin's 1994 anticrime proposal allows police to detain people at will and search homes, offices, and cars without having to demonstrate probable cause.

25. The "*Miranda* warning rules" must be recited to a suspect prior to any questioning.

26. In a police "show-up," the victim or witness is given a series of photographs of possible suspects from which an identification might be made.

27. With respect to nontestimonial exemplars, the Supreme Court has ruled *against* the right to counsel at photographic displays conducted for the purpose of allowing a witness to attempt an identification of the offender.

28. In *Brown* v. *Mississippi*, decided in 1936, the Supreme Court held that physically coerced confessions could not serve as the basis for a conviction in a state prosecution. Just as these confessions could not be introduced in federal criminal trials under the Fifth Amendment, they could not be allowed in state courts under the Fourteenth Amendment's due process clause.

ANSWERS TO THE PRACTICE EXAM

1. d
2. c
3. b
4. d
5. b
6. d
7. e
8. a
9. e
10. a
11. b
12. c
13. c
14. b
15. c
16. c
17. a
18. b
19. F
20. T
21. T
22. T
23. F
24. T
25. T
26. F
27. T
28. T

CHAPTER 9

Beyond the Limits of the Law: Police Crime, Corruption, and Brutality

CHAPTER OUTLINE

I. Police Corruption
    A. Background
        1. Work-related lawbreaking as a problem in every profession and occupation
        2. Wide-spread nature of police corruption
            a. Police Foundation study
            b. Knapp Commission
            c. Mollen Commission
        3. Policing provides many opportunities, temptations, and conditions for corruption.
        4. Police corruption defined
    B. Meals and services
        1. free or discount meals
        2. police presence, keeping officers in and around a business to deter crime
        3. coerced "freebies" as a low-grade form of corruption
    C. Kickbacks, fees for referrals, tow trucks, lawyers, etc.
    D. Opportunistic theft
    E. Planned theft and robbery
        1. direct involvement of police in predatory activities
        2. less likely to be tolerated by police departments than some other forms of corruption

F. Shakedowns, a police officer accepts money from a citizen in exchange for not enforcing the law
G. Protection of illegal goods and activities
H. Case fixing
I. Private security
   1. showing favoritism to some businesses or persons in providing police protection
   2. providing police protection to criminals
J. Patronage, the use of one's official position to influence decision making

II. Explanation of Police Corruption
   A. The society-at-large explanation; the slippery slope hypothesis
   B. The structural explanation
      1. "everybody's doing it"
      2. corruption viewed as a game in which everyone is out to get his/her share
   C. The rotten-apple explanation, a few bad officers in an otherwise honest department

III. Police Violence
   A. A long history of police violence in the United States
      1. A common way of doing police business
      2. public begins to demand accountability, 1960s
         a. criminal law revolution
         b. the Kerner Commission
   B. Police brutality
      1. research by Westley and others
      2. police brutality as a product of norms shared by police in general
      3. the working personality
      4. use of force as a lawful police tool
      5. the watchman style of policing, little training, undefined boundaries and expectations of police behavior
      6. Lindman's explanation
         a. police authority
         b. judgements of social value
         c. police decision making
      7. police authority
      8. judgements of social value
      9. police decision-making
   C. Deadly force
      1. the common law rule permitting deadly force as a last resort
      2. *Tennessee* v. *Garner* (1985)
      3. Fyfe's distinction between extralegal violence and unnecessary violence
      4. over-representation of minorities as victims

IV. Controlling Police Misconduct
   A. Policing the police is difficult
   B. Legislative control
      1. overcriminalization of private conduct

        2. statutes providing a means for citizens to file lawsuits against police officers
    C. Civilian review boards
        1. Waskow's suggestions
        2. efforts in the 1960s to move from internal review to external review of police policy, conduct, and citizen complaints
        3. police resistance
    D. Police control
        1. control of police misconduct from within the department
            a. preventive control
            b. punitive control
        2. history of internal affairs units
            a. "shoo-flies"
            b. late 1940s, Los Angeles, Chief Worton forms the Bureau of Internal Affairs
            c. disliked and distrusted by police and citizens
        3. police professionalism, brutality and corruption are incompetent policing

V. Summary

REVIEW OF KEY TERMS, CONCEPTS, AND IDEAS

Write the definition of the key terms in the space provided.

1. civilian review boards—

2. police brutality—

3. police corruption—

4. "police presence"—

5. police professionalism—

6. *Tennessee v. Garner*—

DISCUSSION

I. Police Corruption

Police corruption has been a problem in the United States for as long as we have had professional police forces. There are several factors which contribute to police corruption, all of which are directly related to the way that police services are organized and delivered in this country. First, the fact that policing is primarily a function of local units of government contributes to police corruption because of the corruption that often exists in city and county politics. Most experts on police corruption acknowledge that illicit police activity is unlikely to flourish in an environment of honest government. The fragmented, locally-controlled nature of police organizations also means that there is no overall "watchdog" authority with broad powers to "police the police."

Second, the fact that American police usually work with little supervision and exercise a great deal of discretion makes it especially easy for a police officer to take a bribe, steal from a burglarized store, or simply look the other way when someone else chooses to be dishonest. Third, the nature of the police officer's job is based on trust. We give police officers the power to deprive us of our freedom, search our homes, and seize our property. We trust that this power will be exercised in an honest and lawful manner, and we assume that it will be.

Fourth, we expect police officers to work in a world of crime, corruption, drugs, prostitution, and violence while remaining pure and unaffected by their working environment. We tend to give police officers the benefit of a doubt when allegations of police misconduct are made, especially when the accusers are criminals, suspected criminals, or persons with somewhat questionable backgrounds.

Finally, the police occupation is largely a closed society. Although this has changed a little in recent years, the "blue curtain" and code of secrecy still protect and hide wrongdoing by police officers. No police officer wants to turn in his fellow cop. He knows that in many situations (some involving life and death), that other police officer may be the only person he can turn to for help.

What do you think is the solution to the problem of police corruption, brutality, and abuse of authority? Given the nature of police organizations in America and the continuing public concern with crime, is it possible to reduce, not to mention eliminate, misconduct by police officers? Is it even realistic to expect poorly paid police officers working in a stressful environment to be free from at least some occasional unethical behavior? Write an essay in which you express your feelings about police corruption and what you think can (or should) be done to control it.

II. Racial Profiling

One of the most controversial issues in policing these days is that of racial profiling. Racial profiling basically means that police employ the tactic of stopping racial and ethnic minorities (primarily African-Americans and Hispanics) moreso than Whites based upon the belief that minorities are more likely to be involved in certain forms of criminal behavior. Police may also stop and question minorities who appear to be "out of place," for example, walking through "White" neighborhoods or driving expensive cars. Critics of racial profiling say that it is nothing more than the employment of old stereotypes which cast minorities in a negative light, that it is an excuse for continuing discrimination and police brutality, and that it violates our Constitutional principle of equality under the law. Defenders of the policy, including many minorities, answer that it is good practice to utilize law enforcement tactics that are based on both hard data and common sense, and that are not designed, per se, to be discriminatory. After all, supporters continue, minorities stand to gain the most when police make stops and arrests based on racial profiling since most of the crime in minority neighborhoods is committed by minorities.

What do you think about racial profiling as a police tactic? Write an essay in which you explain your views, either pro or con. Have you considered both sides of the issue? To help you in your thinking, find and read the following two articles that give opposing perspectives on racial profiling:

(1) "In Defense of Racial Profiling", by John Derbyshire, published in the February 19, 2001, issue of *National Review*, pages 38–40.
(2) "Race and Policing", by Jim Leitzel, published in the March/April 2001, issue of *Society*, pages 38–42.

PRACTICE EXAM

The following practice exam will help you review the key terms, concepts and ideas discussed in this chapter. Give yourself 2.5 points for each correct answer. answers are at the end of the exam.

MULTIPLE CHOICE

1. Many restaurants will offer free meals to police officers for the sake of
    a. earning "points" with the department.
    b. building up a list of favors due them.
    c. "police presence."
    d. avoiding citations for health law violations.

2. _____ can occur when police officers direct individuals in stressful situations to persons who, for a profit, can assist them.
    a. Kickbacks
    b. Patronage
    c. "Police presence"
    d. Shakedowns

3. Opportunistic theft by police typically involves
    a. the pilfering of guns and ammunition from departmental equipment rooms.
    b. the organized taking of drugs and other items from police property rooms.
    c. the stealing of goods from suspects and crime scenes.
    d. all of the above.

4. As a form of police corruption _____ refers to the direct involvement of police in predatory activities.
   a. opportunistic theft
   b. planned theft and robbery
   c. the shakedown
   d. protection

5. _____ is rarely tolerated by police departments.
   a. The shakedown
   b. Patronage
   c. Planned theft
   d. Opportunistic theft

6. Police corruption in the form of "protection" involves
   a. providing bodyguard services to citizens.
   b. accepting bribes from establishments that provide illegal goods and services.
   c. officers perjuring themselves on the witness stand.
   d. the use of police power and authority to influence decision making.

7. The most common form of case fixing by police officers involves
   a. offering perjured testimony.
   b. accepting a bribe in lieu of arresting someone.
   c. traffic ticket fixing.
   d. agreeing to drop an investigation prematurely.

8. _____ involves the use of one's official position to influence decision-making.
   a. Patronage
   b. Case fixing
   c. Bribery
   d. "Bagging"

9. The causes of the urban riots of 1967 were investigated by the
   a. Lexow Committee.
   b. Ranken Committee.
   c. Kerner Commission.
   d. Knapp Commission.

10. William A. Westley's study of police in Gary, Indiana, found "_____" to be the most common response to the question: "When do you think a policeman is justified in roughing a man up?"
    a. "when it is impossible to avoid"
    b. "disrespect for police"
    c. "to make an arrest"
    d. "for drunks and hippies"

11. The most common form of police violence is
    a. brutality.
    b. organized death squads.
    c. the use of deadly force.
    d. *a*, *b*, and *c* above appear with equal regularity.

12. According to political scientist James Q. Wilson, which style of policing is most closely associated with police brutality?
    a. legalistic
    b. professional
    c. watchman
    d. service

13. Most police observers agree that police brutality results from
    a. the right to use force in situations where an officer's evaluation of the circumstances demands it.
    b. elements of the policeman's "working personality."
    c. the police norms of solidarity and secrecy.
    d. all of the above.

14. Sociologist Richard J. Lundman's examinations of policing suggest that brutality is related to, among other things,
    a. the rigid nature of police decision-making.
    b. the cavalier attitude some officers have toward life and death.
    c. police inability to make quick judgments in stressful situations.
    d. police judgements of the "social value" of certain citizens.

15. The common law rule during the Middle Ages authorized the use of deadly force to apprehend a fleeing felon because
    a. felons had no civil rights.
    b. protection of society was of major concern.
    c. all felonies were punishable by death anyway.
    d. the authority of police was unquestionable.

16. Civilian review boards
    a. have reduced police misconduct in every city where they were organized.
    b. were generally supported by most police organizations.
    c. created closer ties between the police and the community.
    d. may be a good thing when public confidence in police integrity has sunk so low that no internal investigative process can ever be viewed as credible.

17. Which of the following areas of investigation does *not* fall within the functions of internal police units?
    a. situations involving the discharging of weapons by officers
    b. allegations of police corruption
    c. allegations of police brutality
    d. allegations by police officers of political harassment by civic authorities

18. The Mollen Commission, convened to investigate corruption in the New York City police department, found that
    a. reports of police corruption were generally unfounded.
    b. corruption was limited to occasional instances of opportunistic theft engaged in by a few officers working alone.
    c. there was a "willful blindness" toward corruption that allowed networks of organized officers to engage in corrupt practices.
    d. there was a sincere effort on the part of supervisors to eliminate corruption from the department's ranks.

19. While corruption is present in many occupations, it is more of a problem in policing because
    a. policing is rich in opportunities for illegal and corrupt behavior.
    b. only corrupt individuals become police officers.
    c. there are relatively few checks placed on police behavior.
    d. police officers are generally low-paid and require other sources of income.

20. Internal policing refers to
    a. control of police misconduct from within the police organization.
    b. the power of police officers to enter private dwellings for the purpose of search and seizure.
    c. James Q. Wilson's "watchman style" of policing that characterizes big city police departments.
    d. allowing citizens on boards or panels to review police misconduct.

TRUE/FALSE

21. It would probably be safe to say that virtually all urban police departments in the United States have experienced both organized corruption and some form of scandal.

22. In a shakedown, police accept money for providing more security or protection than is required by standard operating procedures.

23. According to the Kerner Commission, police patrol practices ranked as the primary stimuli for the urban ghetto riots of the late 1960s.

24. The decision to use deadly force for effecting an arrest is limited to self-defense situations.

25. Research on the use of deadly force by police demonstrates that minority group members are statistically overrepresented among the victims in police killings.

26. The Civilian Complaint Review Board in Washington, D.C. has been heralded as a success by many scholars largely because of the agency's ability to quickly and efficiently process complaints.

ANSWERS TO THE PRACTICE EXAM

1. c	10. b	19. a
2. a	11. a	20. a
3. c	12. c	21. T
4. b	13. d	22. F
5. c	14. d	23. T
6. b	15. c	24. F
7. c	16. d	25. T
8. a	17. d	26. F
9. c	18. c	

CHAPTER 10

The Structure of American Courts

CHAPTER OUTLINE

I. The Evolution of U.S. Courts
   A. Historical role of the courthouse
   B. Growing complexity of the court system
   C. Dual court system

II. The State Courts
   A. State court infrastructure
      1. no two exactly alike—50 jurisdictions
      2. each state makes its own criminal law, law enforcement, and court system
      3. different levels distinguished by jurisdiction
         a. court of last resort (appellate jurisdiction)
         b. intermediate appeals court (appellate jurisdiction)
         c. courts of general jurisdiction
         d. courts of limited jurisdiction
   B. Levels of jurisdiction in state courts; limited, general, appellate
   C. Courts of limited jurisdiction
      1. the entry point for criminal judicial processing
      2. problems include large number of cases and the trial *de novo* system
      3. justice of the peace courts; minimal legal training; often paid from costs assessed convicted defendants; have been eliminated or downgraded in many states

4. municipal courts; urban counterpart of the rural justice of the peace courts; swift, mass processing of defendants; examples of Cleveland and Brooklyn, New York
- D. Major trial courts
  1. authorized to try all criminal and civil cases; courts of general jurisdiction
  2. may be known as circuit courts, district courts, superior courts, or by other titles
  3. judicial circuit; a judge moves from county to county within a geographical area holding court in each one as he/she travels
  4. judges are lawyers, salaried, and full-time
  5. courts of record; written record of the proceedings is kept
- E. Appellate courts
  1. exercise of appellate jurisdiction (reviewing the actions of trial courts)
  2. intermediate courts of appeal and court of last resort
- F. Reform and unification of state courts
  1. recommendations for reorganization
  2. many obstacles to reorganization: political, philosophical, pragmatic; court personnel fear loss of power and status
  3. overloaded court dockets result in congested courts and delayed justice; establishment of special drug courts

II. The Federal Judiciary
- A. unified system based on the Constitution of the United States
- B. administers federal law throughout the 50 states, the territories, and the District of Columbia
- C. U.S. Commissioners and U.S. Magistrate's Courts
- D. U.S. District Courts
  1. created in 1789 by Congress
  2. located throughout the 50 states, the territories, and the District of Columbia
  3. broad jurisdiction over a wide range of cases; courts of general jurisdiction
  4. one or more judges per court; over 600 judges in all; cases may be tried by a judge only or a judge and jury
  5. dramatic increase in workload (cases) in the last 25 years
  6. difficulty of finding qualified persons to serve as federal judges
  7. growing jurisdictional conflicts between state trial courts and federal district courts
- E. U.S. Courts of Appeals
  1. 13 of these, organized in circuits made up of multiple states; also known as Circuit Courts
  2. appellate jurisdiction; cases appealed from the District Courts
  3. cases heard by three-judge panels, or *en banc*
- F. The U.S. Supreme Court
  1. the highest court in the nation- 9 justices serve for life
  2. the origins of the Supreme Court
     a. created by Article III of the U.S. Constitution
     b. early struggle to gain power and prestige
  3. *Marbury v. Madison*
     a. Chief Justice John Marshall
     b. writ of *mandamus*
     c. judicial review

4. judicial scope of the Supreme Court
      a. broad but not limitless
      b. constitutional issues
   5. selection of cases
      a. mandatory review of specified types of cases
      b. writ of *certiorari*; the rule of four
   6. types of rulings- affirm, reverse, remand
   7. growing workload; more petitions for review, fewer cases accepted

IV. Summary

REVIEW OF KEY TERMS, CONCEPTS, AND IDEAS

Write the definitions of the key terms in the space provided.

1. appellate jurisdiction—

2. courts of general jurisdiction—

3. courts of limited jurisdiction—

4. courts of record—

5. dual court system—

6. judicial circuit—

7. justices of the peace—

8. *Marbury* v. *Madison*—

9. Rule of Four—

10. trial *de novo*—

11. U.S. District Courts—_____
_____

12. U.S. Magistrates—_____
_____

13. U.S. Supreme Court—_____
_____

14. writ of *certiorari*—_____
_____

15. writ of *mandamus*—_____
_____

DISCUSSION

I. STATE COURTS

Locate your state's court system on the Internet, and answer the following questions:

1. Does your state have intermediate appellate courts? What are they called?
2. What is the name of your state's court of last resort? How many judges serve on this court? By what method are these judges selected for their positions?
3. By what name are your major trial courts known?
4. Does your state have a "unified" court structure?
5. When was your state's highest court founded?

II. DRUG COURTS

Visit the Drug Courts Program Office at http://www.ojp.usdoj.gov/dcpo/. Explore the Web site and then answer the following questions:

1. What distinguishes drug courts from "regular" criminal courts?
2. Describe the social/criminal context within which drugs courts were born.
3. What are the ten (10) key components of drug courts?
4. Link to the National Drug Court Institute. What is the mission of the NDCI?

PRACTICE EXAM

Take the following practice exam as a way to review the key terms and ideas covered in Chapter 10.

MULTIPLE CHOICE

1. The _____ court system in the United States is characterized by court structures at both the state and federal levels.
    a. dual
    b. hierarchical
    c. appellate
    d. jurisdictional

2. The notion of a dual court system refers to the distinction between
    a. state and federal courts.
    b. inferior and superior courts.
    c. courts of limited and general jurisdiction.
    d. trial and appeals courts.

3. *Misdemeanor, minor,* and *inferior* courts are all courts of _____ jurisdiction.
    a. original
    b. superior
    c. marginal
    d. limited

4. The "jurisdiction" of a court refers to
    a. the geographical area it covers.
    b. the subject matter it deals with.
    c. its place in the hierarchy of the court system.
    d. all of the above.

5. In terms of authority, a court's jurisdiction can be either
    a. general or appellate.
    b. general or original.
    c. limited, general, or appellate.
    d. superior or inferior.

6. Courts of general jurisdiction
    a. process appeals from the trial courts.
    b. are limited in felony cases, to all stages prior to trial.
    c. have the authority to try any case.
    d. have no appellate powers.

7. Which of the following criminal offenses is most likely to be tried in a court of limited jurisdiction?
    a. disorderly conduct
    b. motor vehicle theft
    c. possession and sale of a controlled substance
    d. aggravated assault

8. The trial _____ is a new trial, on appeal from a lower court to a court of general jurisdiction.
    a. *proviso quod*
    b. *nul tiel record*
    c. *de novo*
    d. *per testes*

9. The problems of the lower courts stem from
    a. the volume and nature of their caseloads.
    b. neglect by the higher courts and bar associations.
    c. the trial *de novo* system.
    d. all of the above

10. The jurisdiction of a justice of the peace court is
    a. original.
    b. general.
    c. limited.
    d. appellate.

11. The goals of dedicated drug treatment courts include
    a. linking defendants with community-based drug treatment programs.
    b. the reduction of drug use and recidivism.
    c. avoiding incarceration at all costs.
    d. all of the above.
    e. choices *a* and *b* above.

12. The _____ courts are the urban counterparts of the rural justice of the peace courts.
    a. county
    b. superior
    c. district
    d. municipal

13. Trial courts are "courts of record" because
    a. all felony cases begin there.
    b. a full transcript of the proceedings is made for all cases.
    c. public defenders are available for all defendants.
    d. a record of the accused's case is prepared during the presentence investigation.

14. Courts of appellate jurisdiction
    a. retry lower court cases that resulted in a mistrial.
    b. are limited to matters of appeal and review.
    c. deal primarily with criminal cases.
    d. have a workload as great as the workload of the lower courts.

15. More than half the states have a four-tier rather than a three-tier court system. This additional tier is generally at the _____ level.
    a. trial
    b. lower
    c. general
    d. appellate

16. Currently in the federal judiciary, the U.S. Commissioners
    a. issue search and arrest warrants.
    b. arraign defendants and fix bail.
    c. hold preliminary hearings.
    d. no longer exist.

17. The U.S. district courts are the federal courts of _____ jurisdiction.
    a. general
    b. limited
    c. appellate
    d. misdemeanor

18. There are a total of _____ judicial circuits in the federal system.
    a. 13
    b. 48
    c. 50
    d. 74

19. In the U.S. Courts of Appeals,
    a. all cases are heard *en banc*.
    b. cases heard are those appealed from the U.S. District Courts.
    c. cases heard include those from state appellate courts.
    d. all of the above.

20. The U.S. Supreme Court was created by the
    a. Declaration of Independence.
    b. Constitution of the United States.
    c. Bill of Rights.
    d. Judiciary Act of 1789.

Chapter 10

21. The justices of the U.S. Supreme Court are nominated by the
    a. president.
    b. Senate.
    c. House of Representatives.
    d. attorney general.

22. Supreme Court justices hold _____ terms.
    a. life
    b. 8-year
    c. 12-year
    d. 16-year

23. A case is granted review by the U.S. Supreme Court through the issuance of a writ of
    a. *mandamus.*
    b. *habeas corpus.*
    c. *nolle prosequi.*
    d. *certiorari.*

24. The U.S. Supreme Court has a chief justice and _____ associate justices.
    a. nine
    b. eight
    c. seven
    d. six

25. Who was the first woman to be appointed to the U.S. Supreme Court?
    a. Brooke Taney
    b. Dorothea Dix
    c. Sandra Day O'Connor
    d. Ruth Bader Ginsburg

TRUE/FALSE

26. The mixture of names, functions, and types of state courts seems to have resulted from the fact that each state is a sovereign government in terms of the enactment of a penal code and the setting up of enforcement machinery.

27. Courts of limited jurisdiction are the entry point for most defendants being processed through the criminal justice system.

28. Justices of the peace hear all misdemeanor and felony cases.

29. The U.S. District Courts were created by the Judiciary Act of 1789.

30. A case heard *en banc* is a case heard by a full panel of judges.

31. The U.S. Supreme Court was created by the Constitution of the United States.

32. The justices of the U.S. Supreme Court are nominated by the president.

33. The first chief justice of the U.S. Supreme Court was John Jay.

34. In *Marbury* v. *Madison*, the U.S. Supreme Court gave the president power to appoint Supreme Court justices.

35. The U.S. Supreme Court has appellate jurisdiction only.

ANSWERS TO THE PRACTICE EXAM

1. a	13. b	25. c
2. a	14. b	26. T
3. d	15. d	27. T
4. d	16. d	28. F
5. c	17. a	29. T
6. c	18. a	30. T
7. a	19. b	31. F
8. c	20. d	32. T
9. d	21. a	33. T
10. c	22. a	34. F
11. e	23. d	35. F
12. d	24. b	

CHAPTER 11

Judges, Prosecutors, and Other Performers at the Bar of Justice

CHAPTER OUTLINE

I. Introduction

II. The Courtroom Work Group
   A. Judges
      1. roles and responsibilities
         a. safeguard the rights of the accused and the public
         b. control the flow of cases through the courts; appoint and evaluate court personnel
         c. appeals court judges review and evaluate the decisions of trial courts
         d. influence other aspects of the criminal justice process; probation, pretrial release
      2. selection of judges
         a. federal judges—nominated by the President and confirmed by the Senate—hold office for life
         b. state and local judges—elected or appointed
         c. Missouri Plan—an example of merit selection—an attempt to avoid political influence

3. judicial training
    a. no constitutional or statutory qualifications for serving on the U.S. Supreme Court
    b. all Supreme Court justices are attorneys and have extensive legal backgrounds
    c. state judges—trial and appellate judges are usually lawyers; some in limited jurisdiction courts are not
    d. New York law as an example of statutory requirements
    e. most judges have little or no formal training on how to be a judge; many resist training requirements
B. Prosecutors
    1. roles and responsibilities
        a. enforce the law
        b. represent the government in legal matters
        c. represent the government in matters of legislation and criminal justice reform
        d. plays an important role in every phase of the criminal justice process from the investigation, through the trial, even in parole decision-making
    2. the decision to prosecute
        a. the importance of prosecutorial discretion; virtually unlimited
        b. selective prosecution
        c. many reasons not to prosecute
        d. influences on the prosecutor's discretion; police, defense attorneys, community leaders, etc.
    3. *nolle prosequi*
        a. decision of the prosecutor to "no further prosecute" the case after previously deciding to prosecute
        b. reasons are numerous; evidence problems or plea bargaining arrangements
        c. can lead to abuse, favoritism, and corruption
    4. plea negotiation
        a. primary means by which criminal convictions are obtained
        b. the defendant pleads guilty in exchange for prosecutorial or judicial concessions
        c. advantages for the defendant and the government
        d. plea bargaining is controversial; many objections
        e. U.S. Supreme Court has formally recognized the importance of plea bargaining
        f. plea bargaining as a necessary element of the criminal justice process
C. Defense attorneys
    1. fundamental right of a criminal defendant; Sixth Amendment
    2. functions of the defense counsel
    3. retained counsel
D. Bailiffs, clerks, and other regulars in the American courthouse
    1. bailiffs and sheriffs; maintain order and assist the judge
    2. court clerk; maintain records and process paperwork
    3. court reporters and court stenographers; keep the official record of the trial
    4. witnesses; police, lay, expert
    5. coroners and medical examiners; conduct investigations and inquests, determine cause of death; criticisms of coroner system
    6. auxiliary court personnel; secretaries, investigators, security personnel

III. The Right to Counsel
   A. Narrowly applied to death penalty cases in federal court until the 1930s
   B. *Powell* v. *Alabama*
      1. the "Scottsboro Boys" rape case; convicted and sentenced to death
      2. appealed to U.S. Supreme Court claiming violation of the Fourteenth Amendment due process
      3. convictions overturned; first in a series of Supreme Court rulings widening the reach of the right to counsel in federal and state court
   C. Extending the Sixth Amendment right
      1. *Johnson* v. *Zerbst*; felony defendants in federal court
      2. *Betts* v. *Brady*; noncapital defendants in state court not entitled to appointed counsel if indigent
      3. *Gideon* v. *Wainwright*
         a. U.S. Supreme Court granted *certiorari*
         b. *In forma pauperis*—unable to provide one's own attorney; in the form of a poor man
         c. Supreme Court ruled unanimously in Gideon's favor
         d. counsel in a criminal trial is a fundamental right of due process in state court; felonies
      4. *Argersinger v. Hamlin*—right to counsel whenever defendant may be imprisoned, even in a misdemeanor case
   D. Restrictions on the right to counsel; numerous decisions against extending the right to counsel-attempts by the Supreme Court to maintain a proper balance

IV. Legal Aid, Assigned Counsel, and Public Defenders
   A. Review of legal services for indigent defendants
   B. Voluntary defender programs
      1. charitable organizations, legal aid societies, law school clinics
      2. federal funding support from the late 1960s to the early 1980s
      3. American Civil Liberties Union
      4. weaknesses of this system
   C. Assigned counsel systems
      1. judge appoints an attorney from a list of lawyers in the local community
      2. weaknesses are numerous
      3. advantages—widens the involvement of the legal community in the criminal justice process; brings in attorneys who are outside of the regular courtroom work group
   D. Public defenders
      1. an attorney paid by a unit of government to represent indigent defendants
      2. growing in popularity, especially in medium-and small-sized jurisdictions
      3. several advantages—experience, skill, independent investigations
      4. disadvantages—low salaries, heavy caseloads
   E. Contract systems
      1. attorneys and law firms enter into a contract with a unit of government to provide legal representation to indigent defendants
      2. has yet to gain much popularity

Chapter 11

    V. Legal, Prosecutorial, and Judicial Misconduct
        A. Increasing problem of corruption among judges, lawyers, and prosecutors
        B. The problem of ineffective representation by legal counsel
        C. Judicial discipline commissions and "watchdog" groups and efforts to police court personnel

   VI. Summary

REVIEW OF KEY TERMS, CONCEPTS, AND IDEAS

Write the definitions of the key terms in the space provided.

1. *Argersinger* v. *Hamlin*—

2. *Betts* v. *Brady*—

3. *Brady* v. *United States*—

4. *Gideon* v. *Wainwright*—

5. *in forma pauperis*—

6. *Johnson* v. *Zerbst*—

7. judges—

8. Missouri Plan—

9. motion—

10. *nolle prosequi*—

11. plea negotiation—

12. *Powell* v. *Alabama*—_____
_____

13. prosecutor—_____
_____

DISCUSSION

I. The Superior Court of California, County of Los Angeles.

Visit the Superior Court of California, County of Los Angeles at http://www.lasuperiorcourt.org/, and take a virtual tour of the courtroom. Answer the following questions about the personnel who work in the court:

1. What kind of stenographic machine does the Court Reporter use? How many keys does it have?
2. For which law enforcement agency do Court Bailiffs work?
3. Whose responsibility is it to prepare the official written transcript of the trial?
4. Who arranges for interpreters to assist the court?
5. What are the educational requirements to be a court clerk?
6. How long is the term of office for a trial judge in California?

Now review the Felony Bail Schedule for the Superior Court.

1. What is the presumptive bail on a charge of voluntary manslaughter?
2. What is the presumptive bail on a charge of escape or attempted escape from prison with force or violence?
3. If no presumptive bail is specified, how is bail set?

II. Performers at the Bar of Justice: Federal Judges and Lifetime Appointment.

As discussed in Chapter 11, federal judges receive lifetime appointments to their positions. As long as they hold their office "in good behavior" (a vague expression at best), they cannot be fired, demoted, or otherwise removed from the bench. They cannot have their salaries withheld or reduced. Since they are not elected, as are most state judges, they cannot be voted out of office by the people. The only way to remove a federal judge from office against his or her will is by impeachment, a rarely exercised action. Theoretically, a federal judge could continue to hold office even if he were too senile to find his own courtroom. Is this system a good idea? Why do you think that the Constitution specifically provides for lifetime appointment of federal judges? If you had the power to change the system, would you, or would you leave it as it is? What are the advantages of lifetime appointment? What are the disadvantages?

Write an essay in which you respond to the questions posed in the preceding paragraph.

PRACTICE EXAM

Take the following practice exam as a way to review the key terms and ideas covered in Chapter 11.

MULTIPLE CHOICE

1. Which of the following is *not* a function of trial judges?
    a. issuing and reviewing warrants
    b. ruling on pretrial motions
    c. protecting the rights of the accused
    d. representing the government in matters of law

2. State and local judges are
    a. appointed.
    b. elected.
    c. appointed or elected.
    d. none of the above.

3. The Missouri Plan is a mechanism suggested by the American Bar Association for
    a. controlling judicial discretion.
    b. the merit selection of judges.
    c. reducing "senatorial courtesy."
    d. improving the flow of cases through the courts.

4. Peru's system of "faceless" judges was originally introduced to
    a. reduce the power of several charismatic justices.
    b. inhibit bribes, payoffs, and case-fixing between judges, lawyers, and defendants.
    c. prevent intimidation by terrorists who could identify the judges at public trials.
    d. prevent the media from tracking the decisions of certain controversial judges.

5. The _____ is the top law enforcement authority of a community.
    a. chief of police
    b. chief prosecutor or district attorney
    c. chief justice of the appellate court
    d. sheriff

6. At the most general level, the responsibilities of the prosecutor include enforcing the law and
    a. keeping the peace.
    b. obtaining convictions.
    c. maintaining order under the rule of law.
    d. representing the government in matters of law.

7. The _____ is a formal entry into the record of declaring an unwillingness to prosecute a case.
    a. *non prosequitur*
    b. *non sanae mentis*
    c. *nolens de firma*
    d. *nolle prosequi*

8. The prosecutor has, at least in theory, absolute and unrestricted discretion to choose who is prosecuted and who is not. As such, prosecutorial discretion begins
    a. after a suspect's arrest.
    b. at arraignment.
    c. at the first bail hearing.
    d. during the initial appearance.

9. George F. Cole's study of prosecutors found that
    a. prosecuting attorneys have only a *limited* degree of discretion when deciding whether to bring formal criminal charges against those arrested for violating the law.
    b. prosecuting attorneys have an *unlimited* degree of discretion when deciding whether to bring formal criminal charges against those arrested for violating the law.
    c. prosecuting attorneys have "exchange relationships" with police, defense attorneys, and community leaders, but these relationships infrequently affect the decision to prosecute.
    d. the presiding judge ultimately rules on the decision to prosecute in most cases.

10. It is generally believed that almost 90 percent of all criminal convictions involve
    a. "victimless crimes."
    b. repeat offenders.
    c. negotiated pleas of guilt.
    d. probation.

11. Who plays the major role in the plea bargaining process?
    a. the judge
    b. the prosecutor
    c. the accused
    d. the defense attorney

12. Which of the following is *not* true of plea bargaining?
    a. It reduces the accused's costs of legal representation.
    b. It increases the accused's chances for a reduced sentence.
    c. It more suitably addresses the correctional needs of the bulk of offenders.
    d. It reduces the potential for cases going to trial.

Chapter 11

13. The position on plea bargaining of the National Advisory Commission on Criminal Justice Standards and Goals was that
    a. it should be prohibited.
    b. it should be limited to misdemeanor and nonviolent felony cases.
    c. without it, the criminal process would quickly fall into a "web of chaos."
    d. it should be regulated but supported, since it enables prosecutors to devote more time and resources to cases of greater importance and seriousness.

14. Most defense attorneys have their initial contacts with their clients
    a. immediately after arrest.
    b. during interrogation.
    c. at the initial appearance.
    d. after their clients have been placed on bail or some other temporary release program.

15. Criminal law is a field that
    a. few attorneys actively choose.
    b. has high financial rewards.
    c. attracts many prestigious lawyers.
    d. is a high status segment of the legal profession.

16. In the "lawyer-client confidence game" described by Abraham S. Blumberg, the defense attorney works not only for the client, but also for the
    a. police.
    b. community.
    c. court.
    d. victim.

17. The court reporter
    a. is a liaison between the court and the press.
    b. records and transcribes the text of actions that come before the judge.
    c. has some responsibilities for processing papers executed by the court.
    d. serves as a messenger for lawyers and other court officials.

18. The _____ witness can present as evidence the result of an investigation that led to the arrest of the accused.
    a. lay
    b. police
    c. expert
    d. all of the above

19. Despite the Bill of Right's clear statement guaranteeing the right to counsel, for almost a century and a half after the framing of the Constitution only those persons charged with _____ were actually given this right.
    a. treason
    b. federal crimes
    c. capital crimes
    d. federal crimes punishable by death

20. The case of the _____ reached the U.S. Supreme Court in Powell v. Alabama.
    a. "Sharpesville Fix"
    b. "Scottsboro Boys"
    c. Ku Klux Klan murders
    d. "Zebra" killings

21. In *Johnson* v. *Zerbst*, the Supreme Court held that
    a. in federal cases, the right to counsel becomes applicable upon indictment.
    b. trial judges must inform defendants of their right to counsel prior to accepting guilty pleas.
    c. a defendant's failure to request counsel does not constitute a waiver of his right to counsel.
    d. a defendant has the right to counsel during any police interrogation.
    e. the Sixth Amendment right to counsel applies to all defendants in federal felony prosecutions.

22. The Supreme Court's decision in *Betts* v. *Brady* was overturned by
    a. *Gideon* v. *Wainwright*.
    b. *Powell* v. *Alabama*.
    c. *Moore* v. *Michigan*.
    d. *Johnson* v. *Zerbst*.

23. The decision in _____ established that a defendant has the right to counsel at trial whenever he may be imprisoned for any offense.
    a. *Gideon* v. *Wainwright*
    b. *Kirby* v. *Illinois*
    c. *Argersinger* v. *Hamlin*
    d. *Powell* v. *Alabama*

24. "Indigency standards" refer to criteria used by
    a. the Office of Economic Opportunity to establish the poverty level.
    b. the Department of Health and Human Services to determine welfare eligibility.
    c. the courts to establish bail levels.
    d. judges to determine eligibility for court-appointed counsel.

25. The _____ system is the oldest and most widely used method for the representation of indigent criminal defendants.
    a. public defender
    b. assigned counsel
    c. voluntary defender
    d. legal aid

TRUE/FALSE

26. Appointees to the U.S. Supreme Court must be native-born citizens of the United States.

27. George F. Cole's study of prosecutors found that prosecuting attorneys have only a *limited* degree of discretion when deciding whether to bring formal criminal charges against those arrested for violating the law.

28. Plea bargaining has its advantages for the state because it increases the conviction rate.

29. A defense attorney's most intensive efforts for the accused occur during plea negotiation.

30. Despite its many drawbacks, advocates of the assigned counsel system support it because it disperses the responsibility for defending indigents among a spectrum of practicing attorneys.

31. With few exceptions, defendants who are represented by public defenders are generally more fortunate than those receiving other types of legal services for the indigent.

32. The decision in *Gideon v. Wainwright* extended the right to counsel to indigents in all felony trials.

33. "Three Strikes and You're Out" laws will likely decrease the power of prosecutors because they have less discretion with regard to processing a particular case.

34. The Missouri Plan was structured to upgrade the assigned counsel system for indigent defendants.

35. Under the contract system of indigent defense, law firms or individual attorneys contract to provide services for a specified dollar amount.

36. Over the years Chief Justice Warren Burger has had high praise for the nation's trial lawyers.

37. The major complaint of prosecutors is the lack of prison space.

38. It is the judge that plays the major role in the plea negotiation process.

39. The lay witness is a citizen bystander or victim who has some knowledge relevant to the case.

40. An inquest is a legal inquiry into the cause of a death in which accident, foul play, or violence is suspected.

FILL IN THE BLANK

41. Although all federal judges are nominated by the president, they must also be confirmed by the _____.

42. It is the responsibility of the _____ to maintain order in the courtroom.

43. The decision whether someone qualifies as an expert witness for the defense is made by the _____.

44. The _____ is a licensed physician who is appointed by government authority and carries out the medical aspects of any criminal investigation.

45. The right to counsel is guaranteed by the _____ Amendment.

46. The decision in _____ held that, in the words of Justice Hugo Black, "any person hailed into court (in felony cases), who is too poor to hire a lawyer, cannot be assured a fair trial unless counsel is provided for him."

ANSWERS TO THE PRACTICE EXAM

1. d
2. c
3. b
4. c
5. b
6. d
7. d
8. a
9. a
10. c
11. b
12. c
13. a
14. d
15. a
16. c
17. b
18. b
19. d
20. b
21. e
22. a
23. c
24. d
25. b
26. F
27. F
28. F
29. F
30. F
31. T
32. T
33. F
34. F
35. T
36. F
37. T
38. F
39. T
40. T
41. Senate
42. bailiff
43. judge
44. medical examiner
45. Sixth
46. *Gideon* v. *Wainwright*

CHAPTER 12

The Business of the Court: From First Appearance Through Trial

CHAPTER OUTLINE

I. Is Criminal Justice Chaotic?

II. Bail and Pretrial Release
   A. Bail as a form of guarantee; defendant is set free until trial
      1. dates back several hundred years
      2. freedom under financial control
   B. The right to bail—Eighth Amendment
      1. extent of the right is unclear
      2. federal rule; Judiciary Act of 1789
      3. many state constitutions provide right to bail
      4. excessive bail—*Stack* v. *Boyle* (1951)
   C. Discretionary bail setting
      1. purpose of bail—insure presence of accused at trial or protection of society?
      2. posting bail at the police station; established bail amounts
      3. criteria for setting bail
         a. seriousness of the crime
         b. defendant's prior record
         c. strength of the state's case

D. The bail bond business
   1. ways of making bail; cash or property
   2. bail bond agent; businessperson who sells a service for a fee; nonrefundable
      a. responsible to the court if defendant fails to show for trial
      b. bond agents usually reject poor risks
E. Criticisms of the bail system
   1. results in confinement of low risk offenders
   2. judicial discretion; unreasonably high levels
   3. little background information on accused
   4. bail used as preventive detention
   5. use of bench warrants
F. Pretrial detention
   1. many defendants have trouble making bail set at even a few hundred dollars
   2. failure to make bail results in the defendant remaining in jail
   3. problems of pretrial detention
      a. disrupts employment
      b. mixing of pretrial detainees and sentenced offenders
      c. overcrowding in jails
      d. violence and potential for harm to defendant
G. Preventive detention
   1. high bail set as a means of insuring that defendants do not gain pretrial freedom
   2. legal consequences for the defendant
H. Release on recognizance
   1. Vera Institute—Manhattan Bail Project
   2. release of an accused without requiring monetary bond
   3. based on evaluation of the accused
   4. ten percent cash bond

III. The Grand Jury
   A. A body of citizens authorized to conduct investigations and determine if accused persons should go to trial
      1. dates to 1166 in England
      2. indictment or presentment as an official accusation
      3. the information as an alternative to the grand jury indictment
      4. grand jury provided for in Fifth Amendment to U.S. Constitution
      5. *Hurtado v. California*—grand jury not required in state proceedings
   B. Operation of the grand jury
      1. two types—investigatory and accusatory
      2. special procedures which differ from those used by trial courts
         a. secret proceedings
         b. accused is usually not present
         c. defense counsel is usually not present
      3. true bill—endorsement of the charge made by the prosecutor

C. Grand jury procedure and the Supreme Court
   1. prosecutor directs grand jury proceedings and has wide discretion
   2. the Frank Costello case and indictments based on second-hand information (hearsay)
   3. *United States* v. *Calandra*—exclusionary rule does not apply to grand juries
D. Grand juries on trial
   1. grand jury as a citizen's protection against unfounded charges and prosecution
   2. the ex parte (one-party) nature of the proceeding
   3. abuses in the granting of immunity
      a. transactional immunity
      b. use immunity
   4. the contempt power; used to compel witnesses to testify
   5. an extension of the prosecutor

IV. The Plea; Usually Made at Arraignment
   A. Not guilty—the prosecution must move ahead with its case; standing mute
   B. Guilty—negative consequences; defendant surrenders several rights
   C. *Nolo contendre*
      1. no contest given to the charges
      2. no admission of guilt
      3. cannot be used against the accused in a later civil lawsuit
      4. Agnew case
   D. Insanity plea
      1. admission of guilt with a claim that the defendant is not legally blameworthy because of insanity
      2. dual plea of not guilty and not guilty by reason of insanity
      3. an affirmative defense—defense must enter evidence to support insanity claim
      4. guilty but mentally ill
      5. not commonly used; defendant rarely wins
   E. Statute of limitations
      1. prosecution is prohibited after a certain time period
      2. not applicable in murder cases
   F. Double jeopardy
      1. multiple prosecutions for same offense prohibited by the Fifth Amendment
      2. has taken 200 years to clarify; many U.S. Supreme Court cases

V. Pretrial Motions—Formal Request to the Court for Some Action
   A. Motion for discovery—defense asks to examine the prosecution's evidence
   B. Motion for change of venue—to move the trial to another location
   C. Motion for suppression—to have evidence excluded from consideration at trial
   D. Motion for a bill of particulars—defense request for more details about the charge
   E. Motion for severance
      1. to have multiple charges tried separately
      2. to have multiple defendants tried separately
      3. joinders—when charges and/or defendants are joined and tried together
   F. Motion for continuance—that the trial be postponed for a later date

112 Chapter 12

      G. Motion for dismissal—on the grounds that there is insufficient evidence against the accused to proceed with the trial

VI. Speedy and Public Trial
    A. Sixth Amendment—to prevent the government from delaying indefinitely, especially if the accused is in jail
        1. difficulties in putting this protection into practice
        2. some states have statutory provisions; limits vary from state to state
    B. The Supreme Court and speedy trial
        1. the reasonableness standard; the Constitution is unclear as to meaning
        2. Supreme Court decisions in the 1970s served to clarify somewhat
    C. Speedy trial and the states; made applicable to the states in *Klopfer* v. *North Carolina* (1967)
    D. The Speedy Trial Act of 1974; sets a 100 day deadline between arrest and trial in federal cases
    E. The right to a public trial
        1. origin in English common law
        2. to protect against secret trials

VII. The Jury
    A. Provided by the Sixth Amendment; may be waived by defendant resulting in bench trial
    B. The right to trial by jury
        1. dates back over 700 years; Magna Carta
        2. appears in the U.S. Constitution in both Article III and the Sixth Amendment
        3. federal rule is firm; twelve member juries and unanimous verdicts
        4. not made binding on the states until 1968 (*Duncan* v. *Louisiana*) for serious crimes and 1970 (*Baldwin* v. *New York*) for petty offenses
    C. Jury selection
        1. petit or trial juries
        2. the states may use (and often do) six person juries
        3. eligibility requirements for jurors
        4. voter registration rolls commonly used to select jurors
    D. The *venire*—list of potential jurors who may be called for service
    E. *Voir dire*—to speak the truth
        1. questioning of potential jurors by prosecutor and defense attorney
        2. challenge for cause
        3. preemptory challenge
        4. Supreme Court rulings governing the use of preemptory challenges; problem of excluding minorities
        5. *voir dire* results in a selected jury plus alternates as required by law
        6. selecting jurors by a process of elimination

VIII. The Criminal Trial
    A. Trial begins after the jury is sworn in
        1. question of sequestration
        2. common trial procedures used throughout the United States

B. Opening statements
   1. first by prosecution, then by defense
   2. intended to outline each side's case and preview how the trial will progress
C. Presentation of the state's case
   1. prosecution presents its case first
   2. the rules of evidence
      a. real evidence
      b. testimonial evidence
      c. direct evidence
      d. circumstantial evidence
      e. evidence must be competent, material, and relevant; hearsay not allowed
      f. controversy over use of polygraphs
   3. examination of witnesses
      a. state begins with direct examination of a witness
      b. defense may cross-examine the witness
      c. redirect and re-cross
   4. objections—sustained or overruled
D. Motion for a directed verdict; *prima facie* case
E. Presentation of the defense's case
   1. importance of the "compulsory process" for obtaining defense witnesses
   2. presentation of evidence in chief
   3. privilege against self-incrimination, but accused may testify voluntarily
   4. presentation follows same pattern as the prosecution's case
   5. prosecution retains the burden of proof throughout
F. Rebuttal and surrebuttal—introduction of new witnesses and evidence by the prosecution and defense after the defense rests its case
G. Closing arguments
   1. each side has a chance to make a summation—defense first, then prosecution
   2. the key element is the power of persuasion
H. Charging the jury
   1. the judge instructs the jury on possible verdicts, the rules of evidence, and the legal meaning of "beyond a reasonable doubt"
   2. judge may present a summary of the evidence
   3. instructions can be lengthy and involve complex issues
I. Jury deliberations
   1. jury selects a foreperson
   2. most states require unanimous verdicts
   3. deliberations may be lengthy in order to reach a verdict
   4. the "hung jury"
J. Verdict and judgment
   1. jury presents its verdict to the court
   2. jury nullification—the jury nullifies (cancels out) the force of strict legal procedure
   3. jury may be polled; each juror is asked individually if this is his or her verdict
K. Posttrial motions—to set aside judgment or ask for a new trial

IX. Summary

Chapter 12

REVIEW OF KEY TERMS, CONCEPTS, AND IDEAS

Write the definitions of the key terms in the space provided.

1. bail—
2. *Batson* v. *Kentucky*—
3. bench warrant—
4. *Benton* v. *Maryland*—
5. charging the jury—
6. double jeopardy—
7. *Downum* v. *United States*—
8. *Duncan* v. *Louisiana*—
9. evidence—
10. evidence in chief—
11. grand jury—
12. *Hurtado* v. *California*—
13. indictment—
14. information—

15. *J.E.B.* v. *Alabama ex rel. T.B*—

16. jury nullification—

17. *Klopfer* v. *North Carolina*—

18. mistrial—

19. motion—

20. *nolo contendere*—

21. *Palko* v. *Connecticut*—

22. presentment—

23. release on recognizance (ROR)—

24. sequestration—

25. Sixth Amendment—

26. speedy trial—

27. Speedy Trial Act—

28. *Stack* v. *Boyle*—

29. surety—

116 Chapter 12

30. transactional immunity—_____
   _____

31. true bill—_____
   _____

32. *United States* v. *Calandra*—_____
   _____

33. use immunity—_____
   _____

34. *venire*—_____
   _____

35. *voir dire*—_____
   _____

DISCUSSION

Find a document called "Federal Pretrial Release and Detention, 1996" on the Internet or in your university library. The Web site is http://www.ojp.usdoj.gov/bjs/pub/pdf/fprd96.pdf. Explore the document and answer the following questions.

1. Although the pretrial release decision is up to the court, who may make recommendations to the court regarding whether the defendant should be released or detained pending trial?
2. In what percent of cases was bail required?
3. What was the primary reason (all cases) that federal courts ordered defendants to be detained? How did this vary according to type of offense?
4. What percent of defendants were detained in the judicial district in which you live?
5. Describe the relationship between residence status and percent of defendants ordered detained. Marital status and percent detained. Race and percent detained. Sex and percent detained.
6. Describe the differences between the Bail Reform Act of 1966 and the Bail Reform Act of 1984.
7. How are federal pretrial services administered?
8. What are the two functions of federal pretrial services officers?

PRACTICE EXAM

Take the following practice exam as a review of the key terms, ideas, and concepts discussed in Chapter 12.

MULTIPLE CHOICE

1. The prohibition against excessive bail is guaranteed by the _____ Amendment.
   a. Sixth
   b. Seventh
   c. Eighth
   d. Fourteenth

2. The bail system as we know it today dates back to
   a. well before the Norman Conquest in 1066.
   b. the Judiciary Act of 1789.
   c. the Civil War and Reconstruction.
   d. the Wickersham Commission.

3. A _____ is some third party who posts a bond in behalf of the accused.
   a. realtor
   b. surety
   c. bailiff
   d. bailee

4. The Judiciary Act of 1789 extended the *right* to bail to all
   a. defendants.
   b. federal defendants in noncapital cases.
   c. state and federal noncapital cases.
   d. persons accused of misdemeanors.

5. In matters related to bail, the U.S. Supreme Court has generally
   a. sided with the accused.
   b. sided with the prosecution.
   c. remained neutral.
   d. decided few cases.

6. In *Stack* v. *Boyle*, decided in 1951, the Supreme Court
   a. addressed the issue of "excessive bail."
   b. settled the constitutional status of an accused's right to bail.
   c. held that all offenses are bailable.
   d. ruled that Congress can define which federal offenses are bailable.

7. Which of the following is generally not a consideration in bail setting?
   a. the strength of the state's case
   b. the seriousness of the crime
   c. the safety of the victim
   d. the defendant's prior record

8. Of the following, who are considered the worst bail risks?
   a. first felony offenders
   b. persons whose bail has been set at a relatively low level
   c. prostitutes
   d. repeat offenders charged with minor felonies

9. Which of the following is *not* true regarding bail?
   a. Bail tends to discriminate against the poor.
   b. Bail bond agents have no legal powers over bailed defendants who "jump bond" and flee.
   c. The bail bond industry tends to promote corruption.
   d. First felon offenders are poor bail risks.

10. In many jurisdictions, forfeited bail bonds often go uncollected because
    a. judges realize that collection would wipe out the savings of many poor families.
    b. the machinery for collecting bonds is inefficient.
    c. the courts do what they can to keep the bail bond industry healthy; otherwise, they would be faced with a larger jail population.
    d. all of the above.

11. Research has demonstrated that persons unable to make bail are more likely to _____ than persons receiving pretrial release.
    a. be indicted, convicted, and sentenced
    b. have their bail reduced
    c. receive a lesser sentence
    d. all of the above

12. In the 10 percent cash bond plans,
    a. the court sets bail as it normally would.
    b. the need for a bail bond agent is eliminated.
    c. only 10 percent of the bond must be deposited.
    d. all of the above.

13. The indictment is a charging document based on
    a. the grand jury's initiative.
    b. evidence presented to the grand jury by the prosecutor.
    c. the prosecutor's presentation of evidence to the presiding judge.
    d. a sworn complaint by the victim.

14. A grand jury does *not*
    a. investigate alleged misbehavior by public officials.
    b. find a verdict of guilty or not guilty in criminal trials.
    c. determine if an accused shall be held for trial.
    d. protect citizens from unfair accusations.

15. Since the duties of the grand jury are limited to investigation and accusation
    a. they are of little value to contemporary criminal procedure.
    b. they foster prejudice and corruption.
    c. most prosecutors bypass them.
    d. many of the elements of due process are absent.

16. The "true bill" represents a grand jury's
    a. willingness to rule on a case.
    b. refusal to indict the accused.
    c. endorsement of the charges.
    d. agreement with the prosecutor's "information."

17. In _____, the Supreme Court refused to extend the exclusionary rule to grand jury proceedings.
    a. *Costello* v. *United States*
    b. *Chicago, Burlington & Quincy Railroad* v. *City of Chicago*
    c. *United States* v. *Calandra*
    d. *Hunter* v. *Fogg*

18. _____ immunity prohibits the government from using a witness's compelled testimony at a grand jury hearing in a subsequent criminal proceeding.
    a. Limited
    b. Use
    c. Transactional
    d. Selective

19. When a grand jury exercises its _____, witnesses who refuse to testify may be jailed.
    a. rule of intervention
    b. contempt power
    c. *ex parte* rules
    d. compulsion privileges

20. Refusing to enter a plea results in a plea of
    a. *nolo contendere.*
    b. guilty.
    c. not guilty.
    d. no contest.

21. The protection against double jeopardy is guaranteed by the _____ Amendment.
    a. Second
    b. Fourth
    c. Fifth
    d. Fourteenth

22. In *Palko* v. *Connecticut* in 1937, the Supreme Court
    a. declared that double jeopardy begins at the point where the second jury trial is sworn in.
    b. applied the double jeopardy clause to the states.
    c. rejected the notion that the double jeopardy clause be extended to the states.
    d. held that a state and a city were not separate sovereignties with regard to double jeopardy.

23. A _____ is a formal request to the court for some action, such as an order or rule.
    a. warrant
    b. writ
    c. plea
    d. motion

24. Changing the "venue" of a trial
    a. changes the presiding judge.
    b. moves the trial to some other jurisdiction.
    c. changes the prosecutor.
    d. moves the trial to some other part of the jurisdiction.

25. The Speedy Trial Act of 1974 applied specifically to
    a. noncapital felonies.
    b. federal prosecutions.
    c. felonies under state appellate review.
    d. all of the above.

26. In the _____, the judge rather than jury renders the decision.
    a. trial *de novo*
    b. trial *de juristi*
    c. bench trial
    d. court martial

27. In jury selection, challenges for *cause*
    a. are made by the defense.
    b. are restricted in number by statute.
    c. deal with sound legal reasons for removing potential jurors.
    d. are ruled upon by the bailiff.

28. The purpose of the *voir dire* is to
    a. choose a fair and impartial jury.
    b. educate the citizen as to the role of the juror.
    c. develop juror-attorney rapport.
    d. all of the above.
    e. none of the above.

29. When an objection is "sustained," it is
    a. rejected.
    b. overruled.
    c. contested.
    d. consented to.

30. Should a jury fail to come to a unanimous decision as to the accused's guilt or innocence, the result is a
    a. mistrial.
    b. hung jury.
    c. no bill.
    d. true bill.

31. Jury nullification occurs when
    a. there is a nonunanimous verdict.
    b. there is a mistrial because of jury tampering.
    c. the jury disregards certain aspects of evidence and the law, or suspends the force of strict legal procedure.
    d. the jury is unable to reach a verdict.

32. A motion for a new trial can be based on grounds that
    a. the trial court had no jurisdiction over the case.
    b. there was an error "on the face of the record."
    c. the prosecution was guilty of misconduct.
    d. the verdict included conviction of a charge that was not tested in the indictment.

33. Evidence from which a fact can be reasonably inferred is
    a. testimonial evidence.
    b. real evidence.
    c. circumstantial evidence.
    d. hearsay evidence.

34. The practice of setting high bail in cases where the defendant is considered dangerous is referred to as
    a. pretrial release.
    b. preventive detention.
    c. unconstitutional incarceration.
    d. summary detention.

Chapter 12

35. The _____ established the first release on recognizance program.
    a. American Bar Association
    b. NAACP
    c. Philadelphia Institute of Justice
    d. Manhattan Bail Project

36. An *ex parte* proceeding is a _____ proceeding.
    a. one-party
    b. posttrial
    c. pretrial
    d. bail review

37. Statute of limitations laws vary from state to state but generally do not apply to _____ prosecutions.
    a. misdemeanor
    b. robbery
    c. murder
    d. rape

38. Tire tracks found at the scene of a crime would be considered _____ evidence.
    a. direct
    b. real
    c. testimonial
    d. eyewitness

39. Under the I-bond program, release is prohibited in cases of
    a. aggravated assault.
    b. weapons use.
    c. child pornography.
    d. all of the above.

40. Under "guilty but mentally ill" statutes,
    a. defendants convicted as such go to prison.
    b. insanity pleas have increased.
    c. community psychiatric facilities have become overcrowded.
    d. prosecutors are no longer required to prove insanity.

FILL IN THE BLANK

41. A _____ is a written order, issued by the court, authorizing a defendant's arrest.

42. _____ programs release defendants on their own obligation with no requirement for money bail.

43. The _____ comes from the initiative of the grand jury and is based on its knowledge and observation.

44. The information is a charging document filed by the _____.

45. After the American Revolution, the grand jury was incorporated into the _____ Amendment of the Constitution.

46. In _____, the Supreme Court refused to extend the exclusionary rule to grand jury proceedings.

47. The most common plea at arraignment is the plea of _____.

48. The right to a speedy trial is guaranteed by the _____ Amendment.

49. Evidence is considered _____ when it is legally fit for admission to court.

50. Should a jury fail to come to a unanimous decision as to the accused's guilt or innocence, the result is a _____.

ANSWERS TO THE PRACTICE EXAM

1. c
2. a
3. b
4. b
5. d
6. a
7. c
8. a
9. b
10. c
11. a
12. d
13. b
14. b
15. d
16. c
17. c
18. b
19. b
20. c
21. c
22. c
23. d
24. d
25. b
26. c
27. c
28. d
29. d
30. b
31. c
32. c
33. c
34. b
35. d
36. a
37. c
38. b
39. c
40. a
41. bench warrant
42. Release on recognizance
43. presentment
44. prosecutor
45. Fifth
46. *United States* v. *Calandra*
47. not guilty
48. Sixth
49. competent
50. hung jury

CHAPTER 13

Sentencing, Appeal, and the Judgment of Death

CHAPTER OUTLINE

I. Introduction

II. Sentencing
   A. Sentencing objectives-what is the purpose of punishment?
      1. retribution
         a. make the punishment fit the crime-Cesare Beccaria
         b. desire for proportionality
      2. vengeance
         a. punishment to give society a measure of satisfaction
         b. *Payne v. Tennessee*; U.S. Supreme Court ruling permitting victim impact statements
      3. incapacitation
         a. restraint or isolation
         b. object is community protection
         c. by execution, imprisonment, or exile
      4. deterrence
         a. using punishment to make an example of persons convicted of crimes in order to prevent future crimes
         b. can be either general or specific
         c. most widely held justification for punishment

5. rehabilitation
   a. changing an offender's behavior to prevent future crime—seen as humanitarian
   b. crime has a "cause" which can be identified and corrected
   c. modify behavior and reintegrate the lawbreaker into society
B. Statutory sentencing structures
   1. sentencing philosophy translated into actual punishment
   2. sentencing as a product of the legislature, judge, (sometimes) jury
   3. legislature makes the law
C. Fines
   1. imposed either in lieu of (in place of) or in addition to incarceration or probation
   2. most common for traffic infractions and misdemeanors
   3. can be used for felonies and can amount to thousands of dollars
   4. experiments with use of day fines
D. Imprisonment
   1. various names given to types of prison sentences-three major types: indeterminate, determinate, and definite
   2. the indeterminate sentence
      a. fixed minimum and fixed maximum—no definite time period set
      b. with a range of years, offender must serve at least the minimum
      c. after minimum, offender can be paroled
      d. based on correctional model-rehabilitation philosophy
      e. paroling authority determines when offender is suitable for release—this varies with the individual offender
      f. criticisms of indeterminate sentencing
   3. the determinate sentence
      a. a fixed number of years that the offender is sentenced to serve; may be reduced by parole
      b. may also be known as flat, fixed or straight
      c. court may still give probation or fine instead of imprisonment
   4. the definite sentence; a fixed period of time with no reduction by parole
E. Other sentencing variations
   1. intermittent sentence—a term of imprisonment to be served on certain days as specified by the court, not a continuous time period
   2. mandatory sentence—legal requirement that the judge sentence an offender to a prison term; disallows judicial discretion
   3. mandatory minimums
   4. other alternatives—tailoring sentences for specific crimes and specific offenders
F. Disparities in sentencing
   1. giving significantly different sentences to similar offenders convicted of similar crimes
   2. product of indeterminate sentencing, judicial discretion, and plea bargaining
   3. exists within individual courts and across jurisdictions
   4. examples of research on sentence disparity in various states
   5. consequences of sentence disparity
      a. mocks principle of fairness
      b. judge-shopping
      c. may breed hostility in sentenced offenders
      d. denigrates the image of the courts

G. Sentencing reform
  1. responding to criticisms of sentencing
  2. presumptive sentencing
     a. limited range of years-fixed determinate sentence is set by judge within that range
     b. reduces disparity by limiting discretion and provides community protection
     c. seen as a combination of determinate and indeterminate sentencing
  3. sentencing institutes—to foster interest in sentencing, educate judges, and formulate policy
  4. sentencing councils—panel of judges who review cases awaiting sentencing and make a recommendation to the sentencing judge
  5. federal sentencing guidelines
     a. the U.S. Sentencing Commission created by Congress in 1985
     b. an attempt to produce uniformity in federal sentencing
     c. criticisms related to the separation-of-powers doctrine
     d. U.S. Supreme Court has upheld the Sentencing Commission as constitutional
H. Truth in sentencing
I. The sentencing process
  1. sentencing as a collective decision-making process involving prosecutor, defense attorney, judge, and probation officer
  2. presentence investigation
     a. conducted by probation officer
     b. produces a presentence report
     c. helps judge decide on appropriate sentence
     d. helps in probation and parole supervision
     e. helps in correctional treatment
     f. provides information for parole boards
     g. provides information for research
  3. allocation—right of a convicted offender to verbally address the court prior to sentencing
  4. judge imposes sentence
     a. multiple sentences may be ordered served concurrently or consecutively
     b. jail time; defendant usually has time in jail prior to trial deducted from sentence; "credit for time served"

III. The Death Penalty in the United States
  A. Eighth Amendment ban against cruel and unusual punishment
  B. Brief history of capital punishment in early America—example of New Haven colony
  C. The death sentence, 1864–1967
    1. increase in use of death penalty to a peak in the 1930s-fewer than 200 executions per year by the 1960s
    2. wide number of offenses punishable by death through the 1960s
  D. Capital punishment and discrimination
    1. President's Commission observation that blacks were subject to the death penalty more frequently than whites (1967)
    2. systematic discrimination based on race
    3. Wolfgang and Amsterdam study

E. Cruel and unusual punishment
   1. uncertainty of the meaning of this phrase
   2. *Weems* v. *United States* (1910)—is the punishment disproportionate to the crime?
   3. "The evolving standards of decency that mark the progress of a maturing society" (*Trop* v. *Dulles*, 1958)
F. The death penalty and the Supreme Court
   1. few Supreme Court cases on the death penalty until the 1950s
   2. 1950s and 1960s—NAACP and ACLU legal attack on capital punishment
   3. the 1967 moratorium (period of delay)
   4. significant Supreme Court cases
      a. *Witherspoon* v. *Illinois* (1968)—jury composition in capital cases
      b. *McGautha* v. *California* (1971)—jury discretion in deciding sentence
   5. *Furman* v. *Georgia* (1972)—Supreme Court rules that the Georgia death penalty law was unconstitutional because it was arbitrary, capricious, and discriminatory
   6. *Gregg* v. *Georgia* (1976)
      a. challenge to Georgia's post-Furman death penalty law
      b. bifurcated trial (two-part proceeding-guilt phase and sentencing phase)
      c. structured jury decision-making; mitigating and aggravating circumstances
      d. death penalty is not, in itself, cruel and unusual punishment
      e. in related cases, mandatory death penalty laws struck down as unconstitutional
   7. developments after *Gregg*
      a. *Coker* v. *Georgia* (1977)—death penalty for rape is unconstitutional
      b. *Godfrey* v. *Georgia* (1980)—"depravity of mind"
G. The return of capital punishment; the Gary Gilmore case
H. Methods of execution
   1. majority of the states have capital punishment
   2. hanging, shooting, electrocution, lethal gas
   3. lethal injection ("the ultimate high") as the leading method of execution in the 1990s
I. The death penalty debate
   1. economic argument—is it more expensive to execute someone than to keep them in prison for life?
   2. retribution argument—do some murderers deserve to die?
   3. public opinion—do the American people want the death penalty?
   4. community protection argument—is the death penalty necessary to protect society?
   5. deterrence argument—does the death penalty serve as a deterrent?
   6. irreversibility argument—should we use a punishment that cannot be corrected in the event of a wrongful conviction?
   7. discrimination argument—is the administration of capital punishment fair and just?
   8. protection of the criminal justice system argument—does the death penalty have an undesirable impact on the administration of justice?
   9. brutalization argument—does capital punishment encourage some people to commit murder?
   10. cruel and unusual punishment argument—is the death penalty a violation of the Eighth Amendment?
J. Capital punishment in the 1980s and 1990s
   1. the number of persons on death row continues to grow in the 1990s

Sentencing, Appeal, and the Judgment of Death   129

      2. the number of executions also continues to grow
      3. Supreme Court rulings favorable to death penalty supporters
      4. continuing uncertainty in the minds of the Supreme Court justices

IV. Appellate Review
   A. Appeal—a complaint to a superior court to review a decision by a lower court
   B. Defendant's right to appeal
      1. burden of proof shifts to the defendant
      2. specific rules governing appeals
         a. Plain Error Rule
         b. Automatic Reversal Rule
         c. Harmless Error Rule
         d. Invited Error Rule
   C. Prosecutor's right to appeal
      1. may not appeal a not guilty verdict
      2. may appeal the decision of an appellate court
      3. may be able to appeal to correct legal errors occurring during trial
   D. Appellate review of sentences
      1. sentences are generally unappealable
      2. exceptions noted
      3. U.S. Supreme Court reluctance to question sentences given by trail courts
   E. The appeal process—subject to specific rules of timeliness and procedure

V. Summary

REVIEW OF KEY TERMS, CONCEPTS, AND IDEAS

Write the definitions for the key terms in the space provided.

1. allocution—_____
_____

2. appeal—_____
_____

3. *Coker* v. *Georgia*—_____
_____

4. definite sentence—_____
_____

5. determinate sentence—_____
_____

Chapter 13

6. deterrence—

7. *Furman* v. *Georgia*—

8. *Gregg* v. *Georgia*—

9. incapacitation—

10. indeterminate sentence—

11. intermittent sentence—

12. *Lockhart* v. *McCree*—

13. mandatory sentence—

14. presentence investigation—

15. rehabilitation—

16. retribution—

17. separation-of-powers doctrine—

18. *Tison* v. *Arizona*—

19. truth in sentencing—

20. *Weems* v. *United States*—

21. *Witherspoon* v. *Illinois*—_____
_____

22. vengeance—_____
_____

23. victim impact sentencing—_____
_____

DISCUSSION

Visit the Web site of the U.S. Sentencing Commission at http://www.ussc.gov/.

A. Review the "Overview of the Federal Sentencing Guidelines."
   1. How many levels of crime seriousness are there?
   2. What are "adjustments"?
   3. How many criminal history categories are there?
   4. How is the guideline sentence range determined?
   5. What are "departures"?

B. Follow the "Federal Sentencing Statistics" link to FY 1999, and find your state or federal judicial district.
   1. For which type of crime were most offenders sentenced?
   2. How does your state/district compare with the national figures?
   3. What was the percentage of convictions obtained by guilty pleas compared to trials?
   4. What was the average length of imprisonment for drug trafficking in your state/judicial district? How does this compare to the national average?

PRACTICE EXAM

Take the following practice exam to review the terms, ideas, and issues covered in Chapter 13.

MULTIPLE CHOICE

1. The statement "you are to be hanged not because you have stolen a sheep but in order that others may not steal sheep" is an example of the _____ philosophy of punishment.
   a. retribution
   b. deterrence
   c. isolation
   d. rehabilitation

2. In *Payne* v. *Tennessee* the Supreme Court permitted
    a. prosecutors to appeal an acquittal provided that new evidence was introduced into testimony.
    b. the use of victim impact evidence during the penalty phase of capital trials.
    c. convicted murderers to address the judge and/or jury prior to receiving a sentence.
    d. an offender sentenced to death an opportunity to publicly apologize to his/her victims.

3. The "just desserts" philosophy of punishment
    a. has the object of community protection.
    b. seeks to change the offender's behavior.
    c. suggests the biblical prescription of "an eye for an eye."
    d. implies retribution, vengeance, and revenge.

4. Rehabilitation philosophy is based on the idea that
    a. all persons are inherently evil and must learn to control their evil impulses.
    b. all persons are inherently good and only engage in crime when faced with bad circumstances.
    c. persons who commit crimes have identifiable reasons for doing so, and these reasons can be discovered, addressed, and altered.
    d. criminals are biological inferiors that must be taught how to act in a "civilized" manner.

5. General deterrence seeks to
    a. prevent particular offenders from engaging in future criminal acts.
    b. increase the number of laws so as to reduce crime.
    c. discourage would-be offenders from committing crimes.
    d. restrain convicted offenders.

6. The most widely held justification for punishment is that it reduces crime by means of
    a. deterrence.
    b. incapacitation.
    c. isolation.
    d. rehabilitation.

7. As one sentencing alternative, fines
    a. are never used for felonies.
    b. are imposed either in lieu of or in addition to incarceration or probation.
    c. have never been discussed by the Supreme Court.
    d. all of the above.

8. The philosophy behind the indeterminate sentence
    a. is based purely on a correctional model of punishment.
    b. is essentially punitive.
    c. has little basis in humanitarian ideals.
    d. combines elements of community protection, vengeance, and deterrence.

9. A sentence of 7 to 15 years is an example of a(n) _____ sentence.
   a. intermittent
   b. fixed
   c. indeterminate
   d. indefinite

10. In an indeterminate sentence, the actual amount of time to be served is determined by the
    a. judge.
    b. prosecutor.
    c. jury.
    d. parole authority.

11. A sentence for a fixed period of time with no reduction by parole is a(n) _____ sentence.
    a. indefinite
    b. life
    c. indeterminate
    d. definite

12. Fines calculated as multiples of an offender's daily income are referred to as _____ fines.
    a. indigency
    b. flexible
    c. indeterminate
    d. day

13. Presentence investigations
    a. are mandatory in all jurisdictions.
    b. are useful for determining appropriate sentences.
    c. are of little value for anything other than sentencing purposes.
    d. all of the above.

14. _____ refers to the convicted offender's personal statement to the court prior to imposition of sentence.
    a. The agreement of submission
    b. *Alleviare*
    c. *Crimen trahit personam*
    d. Allocution

15. _____ is the period of detention served prior to sentencing.
    a. "Jail time"
    b. "Time served"
    c. "Dead time"
    d. "Post time"

16. The peak period of executions in America was the
    a. 1930s.
    b. 1940s.
    c. 1950s.
    d. 1960s.

17. Since the *Furman* decision, executions in America have been imposed only for
    a. treason.
    b. homicide.
    c. rape.
    d. kidnapping.

18. An analysis of executions under civil authority in the United States demonstrates that
    a. more blacks than whites were executed.
    b. blacks were executed for rape more often than members of any other group.
    c. the death penalty was apparently an instrument for racial discrimination.
    d. all of the above.

19. Throughout the 1950s and 1960s, which organization was most significant in waging a war against the death penalty?
    a. Congress on Racial Equality
    b. Law Center for Constitutional Rights
    c. Legal Aid Society
    d. National Association for the Advancement of Colored People

20. The Supreme Court ruled in _____ that states cannot exclude from juries in capital cases all persons opposed to the death penalty.
    a. *Witherspoon* v. *Illinois*
    b. *McGautha* v. *California*
    c. *Furman* v. *Georgia*
    d. *Gregg* v. *Georgia*

21. In _____, the High Court held that statutes that leave arbitrary and discriminatory discretion to juries in imposing death sentences violate the Eighth Amendment ban on cruel and unusual punishment.
    a. *McGautha* v. *California*
    b. *Furman* v. *Georgia*
    c. *Godfrey* v. *Georgia*
    d. *Roberts* v. *Louisiana*

22. The High Court's decision in _____ called for a two-part proceeding that would satisfy the constitutional objections noted in Furman.
    a. *Roberts* v. *Louisiana*
    b. *Godfrey* v. *Georgia*
    c. *Woodson* v. *North Carolina*
    d. *Gregg* v. *Georgia*

23. The first person to be executed in the post-*Furman* era was
    a. Luis Jose Monge
    b. Gary Mark Gilmore
    c. Jesse Bishop
    d. Charles Brooks, Jr.

24. Specific deterrence differs from general deterrence in that the former
    a. seeks to discourage others from committing crimes.
    b. is designed to prevent a particular offender from committing future criminal acts.
    c. seeks to prevent violation of specific laws.
    d. is aimed at obtaining social justice.

25. A 60-day sentence served on consecutive weekends is an example of an _____ sentence.
    a. indefinite
    b. indeterminate
    c. intermittent
    d. inconsequential

TRUE/FALSE

26. Statutory sentencing structures designate a range of punishments for specific crimes.

27. The practice known as "judge-shopping" is a result of sentencing disparities.

28. When the framers of the Constitution incorporated the ban against cruel and unusual punishment into the Bill of Rights, what they probably had in mind were the many grisly forms of execution that had appeared in the human history, such as flaying and burning at the stake.

29. Recent demographic statistics of death row inmates reveal that persons on death row are fairly representative of the general population.

30. The decision in *Furman* v. *Georgia* was a statement against the manner in which statutes allowed the death penalty to be imposed.

31. The new "three strikes and you're out" laws that call for life imprisonment following a third felony conviction are an example of an indeterminate sentence.

32. The federal courts have ruled in favor of relying on statistical studies to demonstrate that, at least in a few jurisdictions, the death penalty is more often imposed along racial lines.

33. A conviction can be automatically reversed when major due process requirements were not apparent at trail.

34. The brutalization argument against capital punishment holds that executions increase the homicide rate.

35. In recent years, every poll conducted on capital punishment has found that the majority of Americans favor the death penalty for murderers.

FILL IN THE BLANK

36. A sentence of 7 to 15 years is an example of an _____ sentence.

37. A sentence for a fixed period of time with no reduction by parole is a _____ sentence.

38. The _____ sentence was designed to reduce disparities by limiting judicial discretion without eliminating it, and to increase community protection by imposing a sentence the offender is required to serve.

39. The _____ Amendment bans cruel and unusual punishment.

40. The _____ argument for capital punishment asserts that "the kidnapper, the murderer, and the rapist, as vile and despicable human beings, deserve to die."

ANSWERS TO THE PRACTICE EXAM

1. b	15. a	29. F
2. b	16. a	30. T
3. d	17. b	31. F
4. c	18. d	32. F
5. c	19. d	33. T
6. a	20. a	34. T
7. b	21. b	35. T
8. a	22. d	36. indeterminate
9. c	23. b	37. definite
10. d	24. b	38. presumptive fixed
11. d	25. c	39. Eighth
12. d	26. T	40. retribution
13. b	27. T	
14. d	28. T	

CHAPTER 14

From Walnut Street to Alcatraz: The American Prison Experience

CHAPTER OUTLINE

I. Varieties of Punishment; corporal punishment, death, banishment

II. The Origins of American Corrections
   A. Punishment in the Colonies
      1. ducking stool
      2. stocks and pillory
      3. brank
      4. scarlet letter
      5. bilboes
   B. Punishment versus reformation
      1. punishment as the preferred approach until the 18th century
      2. 18th century (Age of Enlightenment) and the birth of the reform movement
   C. The Classical School of Criminology
      1. A body of ideals for transforming criminal law and procedure
      2. based on the idea that a person is a self-determining, rational, free-thinking being
      3. Cesare Beccaria; the founder of the classical school
      4. Beccaria's *An Essay on Crimes and Punishments*—highlights of the liberal doctrine of criminal law

138   Chapter 14

      5. Bentham, Romilly, and Howard
      6. The pleasure-pain principle; hedonism

III. American Prisons in Perspective; William Penn and the beginnings of American prisons
    A. The Walnut Street Jail
      1. Influence of John Howard
      2. The first American penitentiary
      3. Early model for prisons in America and Europe
    B. The separate system
      1. inmates physically separated from each other by housing them in solitary confinement
      2. inmates were supposed to change through a process of spiritual reflection
      3. virtues of the system
      4. The Eastern Penitentiary as a model prison (Philadelphia, 1829)
      5. the dehumanizing effect
      6. widely adopted in Europe; unpopular in the United States
    C. The silent system
      1. inmates forced to follow a rule of absolute silence at all times
      2. Auburn Prison (New York), 1823
      3. congregate work, hard labor, forced silence
      4. cheaper to build and more productive than the separate system
      5. strict punishment, prison stripes and the lockstep
    D. Prison industries
      1. continuing popularity of the Auburn model
      2. industrial revolution and factory production
      3. contract system of labor
      4. piece-price system
      5. lease system
      6. state account system
      7. state use system
      8. public works system
      9. farming
    E. The Reformatory Era
      1. rise of the treatment philosophy
      2. idea that behavior was not the product of free will; behavior as a product of some pathology that could be corrected
      3. influence of Alexander Maconochie
          a. Norfolk Island
          b. the "mark system" for earning early release
      4. Sir Walter Crofton
          a. the "Irish system"
          b. four stages of treatment
          c. ticket-of-leave as early parole system
      5. the Elmira Reformatory (1876)
          a. Zebulon Brockway
          b. essentials of a successful reform system

            c. Brockway's program (indeterminate sentence, vocational training, etc.) gained in popularity, but reformatory concept failed
    F. The twentieth century industrial prison
        1. prison industry seen as a threat to free enterprise
        2. opposition by unions
        3. federal laws regulating prison-made products
        4. rebirth of reform/rehabilitation movement in the 1960s and 1970s
        5. dissatisfaction with prisons both inside and outside of the walls
        6. efforts to make prisons more humane versus the "law and order" approach to crime

IV. The Federal Prison System
    A. Federal offenders housed in state and territorial prisons through the nineteenth century
    B. Early federal prisons at Leavenworth, Kansas; Atlanta, Georgia and McNeil Island, Washington
    C. New federal laws in the early 1900s mean more federal prosecutions and more federal offenders to incarcerate
    D. 1930—the creation of the Federal Bureau of Prisons

V. Jails and Detention Centers; contrasting jails and prisons
    A. The origins of American jails
        1. jails may date to as early as Fourth century
        2. hulks—ships anchored in a body of water and used as a prison
        3. gaols (jails) of twelfth century England; forerunner of contemporary American jails
        4. disgusting conditions of jails as a consistent theme
    B. Contemporary jail systems
        1. various names—jail, lockup, workhouse, detention center, etc.
        2. all are for temporary or short-term detention
        3. most operated by counties; some by cities (the police lockup)
    C. The jail population
        1. the entrance to the criminal justice system
        2. about 3,500 jails and 605,000 inmates; about 50 percent unconvicted persons awaiting trial
        3. "jail is for the poor, the street is for the rich."
    D. Jail conditions
        1. the jail as a dumping ground
        2. architecture and physical structure
        3. large cells, poor sanitary facilities, lack of adequate staff
        4. the example of Riker's Island (New York)
        5. efforts to improve jail conditions; direct supervision jails
        6. the problem of overcrowding; suggestions for reducing jail populations
            a. more use of ROR
            b. preferential trial scheduling
            c. use of citations
            d. installment plans for fine payment
            e. work-release

VI. Summary

Chapter 14

REVIEW OF KEY TERMS, CONCEPTS, AND IDEAS

Write the definitions of the key terms in the space provided.

1. Cesare Beccaria—_____

2. classical school of criminal law and criminology—_____

3. contract system—_____

4. corporal punishment—_____

5. jails—_____

6. lease system—_____

7. "mark system"—_____

8. piece-price system—_____

9. prisons—_____

10. separate system—_____

11. silent system—_____

12. state account system—_____

13. state-use system—_____

14. "ticket of leave"—_____

15. Walnut Street Jail—_____
_____

DISCUSSION

Review the history of the Eastern State Penitentiary by visiting http://www.easternstate.com/history.html. Answer the following questions about ESP.

1. Describe the floor plan of ESP.
2. Who was the architect whose plan was chosen for ESP? How much was he paid for his work?
3. Who was the first inmate at ESP? Who was the first Warden?
4. When was the first escape from ESP?
5. When was the original prison finally completed?
6. When was the Pennsylvania system of confinement abandoned at ESP?
7. Note the description of Al Capone's cell where he served an eight month sentence during 1929–1930.
8. When did ESP close? What happened to the inmates?
9. Read about the efforts that were made to preserve ESP as a historical landmark in the 1970s and 1980s.
10. What is the street address of ESP? How much would it cost you to take a tour?

PRACTICE EXAM

Take the following practice exam as a review of key terms, ideas, and concepts discussed in Chapter 14.

MULTIPLE CHOICE

1. The modern day counterpart to "banishment" as a form of punishment is
   a. exile.
   b. expatriation.
   c. transportation.
   d. deportation.

2. The colonial device that shackled a convicted slanderer by the feet to a wooden stake was known as the
   a. stocks.
   b. pillory.
   c. bilboes.
   d. brank.

3. Confinement in the _____ in colonial days could be a highly serious punishment because, in addition to the humiliation it engendered, offenders could also be whipped, have their ears torn apart, or even be stoned to death.
    a. pillory
    b. ducking stool
    c. brank
    d. bilboes

4. At the basis of the classical doctrine of criminal law and criminology was the notion that
    a. the criminal law placed restrictions on freedom.
    b. man was responsible for his behavior.
    c. the punishment should fit the crime.
    d. criminal sanctions must not be arbitrary.

5. The major flaw of the classical doctrine of criminal law was that
    a. it made no allowances for mitigating circumstances.
    b. it tended to favor the rich.
    c. it increased the number of punishments.
    d. none of the above.
    e. all of the above.

6. "Hedonism," as it was described in the writings of the classical theorists such as Beccaria and Romilly, referred to the
    a. infamous "bloody codes."
    b. harshness of penalties.
    c. pleasure-pain principle.
    d. pains of punishment.

7. The American prison system was initiated by
    a. John Howard.
    b. Zebulon Brockway.
    c. Homer S. Cummings.
    d. William Penn.

8. Most influential to the beginnings of the American prison experience was (were) the
    a. Pilgrims.
    b. Quakers.
    c. Catholic Church.
    d. Salvation Army.

9. The attractiveness of the silent system was primarily due to its
    a. efficient custody.
    b. economic advantages.
    c. simple architecture.
    d. all of the above.

10. The "lock-step" at early Auburn Prison was
    a. a prison within a prison.
    b. a marching formation.
    c. a security device.
    d. a gate latch.

11. One of the first Americans to implement a reformatory approach to corrections was
    a. Alexander Maconochie.
    b. Walter Crofton.
    c. Zebulon Brockway.
    d. Lewis E. Lawes.

12. The "ticket-of-leave" instituted by Walter Crofton represented the first attempt at what has become known as
    a. parole.
    b. probation.
    c. mandatory release.
    d. bail.

13. During the early decades of this century, there was opposition to prison industries because they
    a. exploited inmate labor.
    b. were threats to free enterprise.
    c. were counter to rehabilitative ideals.
    d. were threats to prison security.

14. During the nineteenth century, federal prisoners were housed in state institutions because
    a. there were so few federal prisoners that separate facilities were not considered necessary.
    b. the only federal institutions were on Indian reservations.
    c. there was only one federal penitentiary.
    d. the existing federal prisons were leftovers from the Revolutionary War and were not fit for human habitation.

15. The result of the convictions generated by the Mann, Harrison, Volstead, and Motor Vehicle Theft Acts was
    a. a reduction in the number of federal offenders.
    b. the crime wave of the 1930s.
    c. a new federal crime code.
    d. the creation of the Federal Bureau of Prisons.

16. Alcatraz Island Penitentiary was
    a. the most repressive maximum security prison in the nation.
    b. the model prison of the federal system.
    c. an effective deterrent for incorrigible criminals.
    d. an example of the "best" and the "worst" of American prisons.

17. The American jail population is composed primarily of
    a. women.
    b. convicted felons awaiting sentence.
    c. unarraigned defendants.
    d. arrestees with histories of drug abuse.

18. Recent data describing the characteristics of inmates of local jails suggest that these detainees
    a. are more often black than white.
    b. are primarily the most indigent of defendants.
    c. have, in most instances, less than an eighth grade education.
    d. all of the above.

19. The American prison system began in the city of
    a. Boston.
    b. New York.
    c. Richmond.
    d. Baltimore.
    e. Philadelphia.

20. Under the lease system of prison labor,
    a. contractors assumed complete control over inmates.
    b. only the inmates' work was supervised by the contractors.
    c. most work was in the area of manufacturing.
    d. manufactured goods were sold on the open market.

FILL IN THE BLANK

21. The beginnings of the classical school of criminal law and criminology can be attributed to the work of _____.

22. _____ was America's first penitentiary.

23. The idea behind the _____ system was that confinement in an isolated cell would give the convict an opportunity to contemplate the evils of his past life, thereby leading him to resolve to reform his future conduct.

24. Under Alexander Maconochie's _____ at Norfolk Island, an inmate could earn early release by hard work and good behavior.

25. _____ are facilities of local authority used for temporary detention.

ANSWERS TO THE PRACTICE EXAM

1. d
2. c
3. a
4. b
5. a
6. c
7. d
8. b
9. b
10. b
11. c
12. a
13. b
14. a
15. d
16. a
17. d
18. b
19. e
20. a
21. Cesare Beccaria
22. The Walnut Street Jail
23. separate
24. "mark system"
25. Jails

CHAPTER 15

Penitentiaries, Prisons, and Other Correctional Institutions: A Look Inside the Inmate World

CHAPTER OUTLINE

I. Total Institutions

II. Types of Prisons
   A. Maximum-security prisons
      1. for the most aggressive and incorrigible inmates
      2. emphasize custody and control
      3. physical features—walls, wire, and towers
      4. inside cell design; cell blocks
      5. designed to prevent escapes
      6. increasing use of technology
   B. Supermax prisons—high custody housing units
   C. Medium-security prisons
      1. less emphasis on physical control features than maximum-security
      2. outside cell design
      3. inmates are considered less dangerous and less likely to escape

    D. Minimum-security prisons
        1. for low-risk inmates
        2. few, if any, fences
        3. cottage-style housing
    E. Open institutions—prisons without walls
        1. farms, ranches, camps
        2. less costly to operate than traditional prisons

III. Correctional Organization and Administration; early 20th century
    A. Prison administration
        1. two primary systems for organizing prisons statewide (Department of Correction model)
        2. Commissioner, Director, or Secretary as top official of DOC
        3. Individual prisons headed by warden or superintendent
            a. job is to manage the prison
            b. deputy or assistant wardens
            c. various methods or selecting wardens
    B. Prison personnel
        1. professional staff—psychologists, physicians, chaplains, etc.
        2. custodial staff
        3. guards redefined as correctional officers
        4. negative stereotype of correctional officers
        5. difficult nature of correctional officer's job
        6. mechanisms for maintaining order
        7. different types of officers; different working styles

IV. Institutional Routines
    A. Prison facilities; many are old and overcrowded
    B. Classification
        1. evaluate incoming inmates; determine security and treatment needs
        2. past systems of classification
        3. reception and orientation units
        4. classification committee
        5. reception centers
        6. problems with classification
        7. classification process
        8. trends in classification
    C. Prison programs
        1. health and medical services
            a. wide range of services
            b. contract medical services
            c. inmate medical history—drugs, alcohol, poor diet
        2. religious programs
            a. long history in American prisons
            b. chaplain's role
            c. criticisms of religious programs

3. education programs; academic and vocational; may reduce recidivism
4. prison labor and industry
   a. inmates can develop skills, make money, have something to do
   b. not enough programs to meet the needs
   c. program examples
5. clinical treatment programs
   a. education and training as rehabilitation
   b. counseling
   c. social casework
   d. psychological and psychiatric services
   e. group treatment programs
6. drug abuse treatment; therapeutic community

V. Prison Discipline
   A. Rules and regulations
      1. for safe and orderly operation of the prison
      2. to provide a routine
      3. "convict bogey"
   B. Contraband
   C. Rule violations

VI. Sex in Prison
   A. Same gender sex
      1. prisons as single sex institutions
      2. research in Delaware
      3. prostitution and forced sex
      4. sex in women's prisons
   B. Sexual assault
      1. homosexual rape
      2. rape and coerced sex in women's prisons
      3. abuses in Georgia
      4. homosexual rape as a power play
   C. Conjugal visitation
      1. long history in U.S., Europe, Latin America
      2. arguments for and against
      3. conjugal visitation and women's prisons
      4. the problem of AIDS
   D. Coeducational prisons
      1. men and women eat and work together, but live separately
      2. creates a more normal living environment
      3. can have negative outcomes; uncertain future

Chapter 15

VII. The Inmate Social System; emphasis on custody and security
   A. Prisonization
      1. the prison community; norms and values
      2. Clemmer's research in the 1930s
      3. prisonization as criminalization
   B. Inmate code
      1. expression of inmate subculture
      2. serves to unify inmates against staff
   C. Sources and functions of the inmate social system
      1. deprivation or importation?
      2. mechanism for controlling inmate behavior
      3. inmate and staff accommodation

VIII. Women in Prison
   A. Women's institutions
      1. women are about 7% of national inmate population
      2. 1873—first separate prison for women in U.S. (Indiana)
      3. variety of institutions
      4. few treatment programs; many emphasize "women's work"
   B. Women and children in prison
      1. new efforts to increase contact with children
      2. extended visits for children
      3. helps women adjust to prison and function better upon release
   C. The social order of women's prisons
      1. limited research
      2. characteristics of women inmates
      3. cottage system of housing
      4. compared to men's prisons; similarities and differences

IX. The Effectiveness of Correctional Treatment
   A. Early attempts; Cambridge-Somerville Youth study
   B. Martinson Report
      1. evaluation of prison treatment programs
      2. "what works?"; confirmed earlier studies; media attention; criticism
   C. Obstacles to effective correctional treatment

X. Summary

REVIEW OF KEY TERMS, CONCEPTS, AND IDEAS.

Write the definitions for the key terms in the space provided.

1. classification—_____
_____

2. conjugal visitation—

3. inmate code—

4. inside cells—

5. maximum-security prisons—

6. open institutions—

7. prisonization—

8. reception center—

9. shock incarceration—

10. supermax prisons—

11. total institutions—

DISCUSSION

Read the following scenario, think about your various options, and decide what you would do in this situation. Consider all possible outcomes, and what you may stand to gain or lose as a result of your decision. Write an essay in which you explain why you chose this particular course of action.

You have been a correctional officer at Central State Prison for six months. This is your first job since you graduated from college, and since you have chosen corrections as a career, you want to get off to a good start. You realize that with your education you have a good shot at moving up the ranks quickly. Your supervisor, SGT Ross, has commented several times that you are a quick learner and that he is impressed with your work. You just received your first personnel evaluation, and your scores were good enough to get you noticed by the warden.

While on duty one evening in C Cellhouse, you overhear loud voices coming from the TV room. Thinking that there may be a problem, you head in that direction. Just as you walk through the door, you observe inmate Jones land a fist to the nose of inmate Wilson; Wilson appears to be "out" when he hits the floor. You go ahead and enter the room and say, "Hey, what's going on here?" Just then you notice SGT Ross standing in the corner of the room with his arms folded across his chest, grinning.

"No problem," Ross says, "these guys were just settling a little disagreement." Wilson seems to have regained his senses, but is still on the floor moaning in obvious pain. SGT Ross continues, "Jones here was getting a little tired of Wilson trying to force him into the White Arian Rangers."

You know that the White Arian Rangers is the most feared white gang in the prison, and that WARs are suspected of several inmate murders. Wilson is believed to be a top "officer" in the White Arian Rangers. You also know that Jones has a clean record. He is a quiet inmate who is doing time for robbery. He is generally respectful of correctional staff and tends to avoid trouble-making inmates.

"Let's go" says SGT Ross, "we need to get ready for the 8:00 PM count."

Prison policy requires that a written incident report be filed in this situation so you say to SGT Ross: "You want to do the report, or do you want me to do it?"

"What report?" he replies, with a smile. "What incident? I didn't see anything, did you?"

PRACTICE EXAM

Take the following practice exam as a way to review to terms, ideas, and concepts in Chapter 15.

MULTIPLE CHOICE

1. _____ house the most serious offenders and are characterized by double and triple security patterns.
    a. High-security prisons
    b. Maximum-security prisons
    c. Reformatories
    d. Penitentiaries

2. _____ are constructed back to back, with corridors running along the outside of the cell house.
    a. Inside cells
    b. Cell blocks
    c. Outside cells
    d. Cell tiers

3. Which of the following statements about contemporary prison administration is incorrect?
   a. Prisons are often organized as a subdivision of some larger branch of state government.
   b. Most wardens are career civil service employees.
   c. Most wardens are highly educated in the behavioral sciences.
   d. The management of a prison is a major administrative task similar to running a large business.

4. In prison academic education programs, the emphasis is on:
   a. learning how to cope with prison life.
   b. gaining basic knowledge and communication skills.
   c. preparing inmates for post-release employment.
   d. helping inmates earn a college degree.

5. Which of the following are typically viewed as the primary rehabilitative tools a correctional institution has to offer?
   a. academic education and vocational training
   b. clinical treatment programs
   c. integrated medical and recreation programs
   d. carefully constructed psychotherapy programs

6. Which of the following statement about prison vocational programs is inaccurate?
   a. Vocational programs are often poorly equipped.
   b. Vocational programs often emphasize training in fields where jobs are scarce on the outside.
   c. Inmates receive training in areas that are relevant to the outside job market.
   d. Programs often lack adequate technical staff.

7. The therapeutic community is a:
   a. form of institutionalized group therapy.
   b. total treatment environment.
   c. variety of group social casework.
   d. form of group psychotherapy.

8. Which of the following statements about conjugal visitation is inaccurate?
   a. It is generally available only to male inmates.
   b. It may help to preserve marriages.
   c. It tends to place strains on the family unit because of the environment of the visit.
   d. It reduces homosexuality.

9. The primary task of prisons is:
   a. treatment.
   b. punishment.
   c. rehabilitation.
   d. custody.

Chapter 15

10. The Martinson Report on the effectiveness of correctional treatment:
    a. said little that had not already been said before.
    b. said that with few and isolated exceptions, prison treatment programs had little effect on recidivism.
    c. pushed researchers to improve their studies of prison treatment programs.
    d. all of the above.

TRUE/FALSE

11. Contemporary correctional officers often feel that their authority has been taken away from them and that inmates have all the power.

12. The major rule violations that occur in prisons usually involve drugs, sex, and fighting.

13. The experiments with co-educational prisons conducted so far have not been especially encouraging.

14. The inmate social system is an effective mechanism for controlling inmate behavior.

15. Shock incarceration can be an effective alternative to traditional prisons for first-time offenders.

FILL IN THE BLANK

16. _____ is a process through which the educational, vocational, treatment, and custodial needs of the offender are determined.

17. Any item that is not authorized or issued in a prison is known as _____

18. The Martinson Report was a study of prison _____.

19. _____ institutions prohibit interaction with the larger "outside" world.

20. _____ is the process observed by Donald Clemmer by which inmates learn the values, customs, and behaviors of the inmate subculture.

ANSWERS TO THE PRACTICE EXAM

1. b
2. a
3. c
4. b
5. a
6. c
7. b
8. c
9. d
10. d
11. F
12. T
13. F
14. T
15. F
16. Classification
17. contraband
18. treatment programs
19. Total
20. Prisonization

CHAPTER 16

Prison Conditions and Inmate Rights

CHAPTER OUTLINE

I. Introduction
    A. Inmates as "slaves of the state"
    B. The "hands-off" doctrine
    C. The beginnings of the prisoners' rights movement

II. Attica, 1971
    A. Conditions at Attica
        1. for inmates
            a. mail and reading material restricted
            b. 14–16 hours per day in the cell
            c. tight regulations and many petty rules
        2. for officers
            a. monotonous work
            b. culture conflict with inmates
            c. frustration, tension, and fear
        3. Racism, fueled by conflict between the races outside the walls
    B. The revolt
        1. growing tensions between officers and inmates
        2. precipitating incidents

C. The assault
1. failed negotiations
2. assault by state police
3. 10 officer hostages and 29 inmates killed, all by state police gunfire

III. In Pursuit of Prisoners' Rights
A. The traditional view of inmates and the reluctance of the courts to intervene in prison affairs
B. The Writ of *Habeas Corpus*
1. challenging the lawfulness of confinement
2. extended to challenging the *conditions* of confinement
C. Civil rights and prisoners, rights
1. Civil Rights Act of 1871 (Section 1983)
2. *Monroe* v. *Pape* (1961), citizens can sue state officials in federal court for violation of civil rights
3. later Supreme Court rulings apply to prison inmates
4. does not require exhaustion of state remedies and can result in monetary damages

IV. Legal Services in Prison
A. *Ex parte Hull* (1941), inmate access to the courts
B. *Johnson* v. *Avery* (1969)
1. absence of *meaningful* access to the courts
2. the rise of "jailhouse lawyers"
3. in the absence of alternative legal services, jailhouse lawyers must be permitted to assist inmates seeking postconviction relief
4. subsequent decisions in the 1970s
C. Jailhouse lawyers
1. perceived threats to prison administration
2. the continuing significant role of jailhouse lawyers

V. Constitutional Rights and Civil Disabilities
A. Bills of attainder, prohibited by the U.S. Constitution
B. Civil death, the loss of all civil rights
C. Religion
1. traditionally encouraged or even required
2. the Black Muslim movement of the 1960s
D. Mail and media interviews
1. restrictions on mail to prevent trafficking in contraband, prevent communication concerning escape plots, etc.
2. U.S. Supreme Court rulings in the 1970s limited prison officials, power to totally restrict inmate mail communication (*Procunier* v. *Martinez*, 1974)
3. The "reasonableness" standard replaces the "substantial government interest" standard in 1989 (*Thornburgh* v. *Abbott*)

E. Rehabilitative services
   1. rehabilitative treatment is not a constitutional right
   2. restrictions on rehabilitative practices that seem more like punishment (*A Clockwork Orange*)
   3. some treatment programs may be mandatory (education, mental illness)
F. Medical services
   1. *Estelle* v. *Gamble*, 1976, deliberate indifference
   2. prison responses to HIV/AIDS
G. Prisoner labor unions, no constitutional right to form a union

VI. Prison Discipline and Constitutional Rights
   A. Papillon and the French penal colonies
   B. The Arkansas prison scandal
      1. abuses of inmates, "The Tucker Telephone"
      2. Thomas O. Merton
      3. the trusty system
      4. corruption exposed to the press in 1968
      5. Arkansas prison system declared unconstitutional in 1970, *Holt* v. *Sarver*
   C. Solitary confinement
      1. traditional means of disciplining inmates
      2. solitary confinement is not unconstitutional, certain conditions of confinement may be unconstitutional
   D. The Lash, *Jackson* v. *Bishop* (1968), whipping is in violation of the Eighth Amendment
   E. Prison disciplinary proceedings
      1. traditionally arbitrary administrative operations controlled by wardens
      2. requirement for due process, *Wolff* v. *McDonnell* (1974)

VII. The Conditions of Incarceration
   A. Prisons should not impose punishment of a barbaric nature above and beyond incarceration
   B. The Texas prison suit
      1. Texas prisons in the 1970s
      2. the problem of overcrowding
      3. breakdown of control in the early 1980s
      4. *Ruiz* v. *Estelle* (1980), Texas system declared unconstitutional
   C. The New Mexico inmate massacre
   D. Future prospects
      1. continuing problems related to overcrowding and poor prison conditions
      2. the riots at Deer Lodge, Montana (1991), and Lucasville, Ohio (1993)
      3. lockdowns used to confine inmates around the clock as a control device
      4. continuing problems at Attica and New Mexico State Penitentiary

VIII. Reform Versus Law and Order
   A. The prison dilemma of the 1990s, increasing inmate rights and unprecedented growth in prison populations
   B. *Rhodes* v. *Chapman* (1981), double-celling is not unconstitutional considering "totality of circumstances"

Chapter 16

    C. *Hudson* v. *Palmer*, (1984), inmates have no Fourth Amendment protection
    D. *Wilson* v. *Seiter*, (1991), inmate must prove "deliberate indifference" by prison officials when alleging that confinement violates the Eighth Amendment
    E. Privatization of corrections, prisons built and operated by private business

REVIEW OF KEY TERMS, CONCEPTS, AND IDEAS

Write the definitions for the key terms in the space provided.

1. civil death—
2. *Estelle* v. *Gamble*—
3. *habeas corpus*—
4. "hands-off" doctrine—
5. *Holt* v. *Sarver*—
6. *Hudson* v. *Palmer*—
7. injunctive relief—
8. *Jackson* v. *Bishop*—
9. *Johnson* v. *Avery*—
10. *Jones* v. *North Carolina Prisoners' Labor Union*—
11. lockdown—
12. *Monroe* v. *Pape*—

13. privatization of corrections—_____
   _____

14. *Procunier* v. *Martinez*—_____
   _____

15. *Rhodes* v. *Chapman*—_____
   _____

16. *Ruiz* v. *Estelle*—_____
   _____

17. Section 1983—_____
   _____

18. *Thornburgh* v. *Abbott*—_____
   _____

19. *Wilson* v. *Seiter*-—_____
   _____

20. *Wolff* v. *McDonnell*-—_____
   _____

DISCUSSION

Locate a publication called "Challenging the Conditions of Prisons and Jails: A Report on Section 1983 Litigation," and answer the following questions. The report may be located by visiting the Bureau of Justice Statistics Web site at http://www.ojp.usdoj.gov/bjs/welcome.html, or it may be available in the government documents section of your university library.

1. How was the research on Section 1983 lawsuits for this report conducted?
2. Find your state on Table 1. How many Section 1983 lawsuits were filed in your state in 1991? What was the rate per 1000 prisoners?
3. The central conclusion of this study was that "there are important gradations in Section 1983 litigation." What does this statement mean?
4. According to the report, "courts must balance prisoners' constitutional rights against the fundamental interests of prisons and jails." What are the three "fundamental interests" indentified?
5. According to Table 3, what are the top three most common issues raised by inmates in Section 1983 lawsuits?
6. Table 4 describes the manner of disposition of Section 1983 lawsuits. What does "disposition" mean in this context? What percentage of cases actually make it all the way to a trial verdict?
7. Inmates are not entitled to legal counsel in Section 1983 lawsuits—explain why.

8. Although inmates occasionally "win" Section 1983 lawsuits, and occasionally receive monetary rewards, these awards are typically smaller that the multi-million dollar awards that are publicized in the media. What are the two reasons for the disparity between what usually happens and what is reported in the press?

PRACTICE EXAM

Take the following practice exam in order to review some of the key words, terms, and ideas presented in Chapter 16.

MULTIPLE CHOICE

1. Under the "hands-off" doctrine, the Supreme Court (prior to the 1960s) refused to consider inmate complaints regarding:
    a. the fitness of prison environments.
    b. the abuse of administrative authority.
    c. the constitutional deprivations of prison life.
    d. the general conditions of incarceration.
    e. all of the above.

2. The riot at New York's Attica Prison in 1971 was the result of
    a. the "Dewer incident."
    b. daily degradation and humiliation.
    c. the desire to escape.
    d. a barbaric custodial staff.

3. *Habeas corpus* is a Latin term meaning
    a. "call up the record."
    b. "I do not contest."
    c. "you should have the body."
    d. "release the accused."

4. After *Coffin* v. *Reichard* in 1944, the writ of *habeas corpus* could be used by inmates to challenge the
    a. conditions of confinement.
    b. fairness of long sentences.
    c. limits of due process.
    d. legality of incarceration.

5. The specific vehicle that opened the federal courts to inmates confined in state institutions to challenge the conditions of prison life was
    a. *Coffin* v. *Reichard*.
    b. the Federal *Habeas Corpus* Act.
    c. Article III of the Constitution.
    d. Section 1983 of the Civil Rights Act of 1871.

6. The decision in _____ permitted citizens to bring Section 1983 suits against state officials to the federal courts, without first exhausting state judicial remedies.
   a. *Monroe* v. *Pape*
   b. *Preiser* v. *Rodriguez*
   c. *Ruffin* v. *Commonwealth*
   d. *Holt* v. *Sarver*

7. The decision in *Johnson* v. *Avery* dealt with
   a. legal services in prison.
   b. the right to treatment.
   c. prison religious services.
   d. prison discipline.

8. "Civil death" refers to
   a. "bills of attainder."
   b. the loss of freedom.
   c. the loss of all civil rights.
   d. the loss of the right to vote.

9. In the case of _____ the Black Muslim faith was declared a genuine religion whose members are allowed to hold services in prisons.
   a. *Fulwood* v. *Clemmer*
   b. *Jones* v. *Willingham*
   c. *Northern* v. *Nelson*
   d. *Long* v. *Parker*

10. _____ was the only case involving the religious rights of prisoners ever to reach the U.S. Supreme Court.
    a. *Cruz* v. *Beto*
    b. *Long* v. *Parker*
    c. *Fulwood* v. *Clemmer*
    d. *Rolando* v. *del Carmen*

11. Opposition to the Black Muslims' right to hold religious services in prison was based primarily on
    a. discrimination against blacks.
    b. the notion that the Black Muslim faith was not a "religion."
    c. the belief that assemblage of Black Muslims would be revolutionary in character and would present dangers to security.
    d. the conviction that only the more conventional religions taught beliefs that were in line with prison philosophy.

162 Chapter 16

12. The issue in question in *Wolff* v. *McDonnell* was
    a. whether or not prison officials can open correspondence from an inmate's attorney.
    b. whether or not prison mail censorship is constitutional.
    c. whether or not prison officials can refuse to mail correspondence that makes negative statements about prison administration.
    d. whether or not prison officials can ban inmates from having interviews with the media.

13. The discussion in the textbook about Anthony Burgess' book *A Clockwork Orange* related to prison
    a. medical malpractices.
    b. disciplinary practices.
    c. solitary confinement.
    d. rehabilitative practices.

14. Beyond its ruling in _____ the Supreme Court has generally left the specifics of the medical rights of prison inmates to the lower courts.
    a. *Wilson* v. *Kelley*
    b. *Estelle* v. *Gamble*
    c. *Padgett* v. *Stein*
    d. *Huxley* v. *Burgess*

15. In the Arkansas prison system of the 1960s, the "Tucker telephone" was
    a. a standard prison intercom used to send messages to the warden.
    b. an instrument of torture.
    c. a signal device used to warn inmates that guards were approaching.
    d. a contraption used in a prison-wide lottery system.

16. The entire Arkansas prison system was declared in violation of the Eighth Amendment by
    a. *Ruiz* v. *Estelle.*
    b. *Holt* v. *Sarver.*
    c. *Jackson* v. *Bishop.*
    d. *Tucker Prison Farm* v. *Brubaker.*

17. The end of whipping as an official means of enforcing prison rules was the result of the decision in
    a. *Jackson* v. *Bishop.*
    b. *Holt* v. *Sarver.*
    c. *State* v. *Canon.*
    d. *Wolff* v. *McDonnell.*

18. Silberman's study of inmate access to attorneys, law libraries, and formal adjudication mechanisms found that
    a. access of this kind contributed to an increase in disputes and lawsuits filed by inmates against correctional officers, prison administrators, and other inmates.
    b. these resources appeared to reduce inmate alienation and reliance on violent self-help.
    c. access of this kind often served to further aggravate existing prison conflicts.
    d. choices *a* and *c* above.

19. Perhaps the most savage prison riot in U.S. history occurred in 1980 at
    a. Attica Prison.
    b. Arkansas State Penitentiary.
    c. New Mexico State Penitentiary.
    d. the State Prison of Southern Michigan.

20. In *Rhodes* v. *Chapman*, the ruling involved
    a. double-celling
    b. inmate violence
    c. medical services
    d. solitary confinement

TRUE/FALSE

21. The "hands-off" doctrine maintained by the courts for so many decades relates to their refusal to deal with inmate complaints.

22. Traditionally, the writ of *habeas corpus* was limited to contesting the conditions of incarceration.

23. The decision in *Avery* v. *Johnson* dealt with prison religious services.

24. Inmates who assist other inmates in the preparation of legal documents are known as jailhouse lawyers.

25. "Civil death" refers to the loss of freedom.

26. The issue in question in *Wolff* v. *McDonnell* was whether or not prison officials can refuse to mail correspondence that makes negative statements about prison administration.

27. The leading Supreme Court case concerning the Black Muslim movement was *Cruz* v. *Beto*.

28. In *Estelle* v. *Gamble*, the Supreme Court ruled that deliberate indifference to the serious medical needs of prisoners violates the Eighth Amendment.

29. On the issue of solitary confinement, the courts have ruled that sanitary facilities must be available, and that the presence of mice and roaches is an undue health hazard.

30. A lockdown is a situation in which inmates are locked in their cells around the clock.

31. The two problems that seem to be most common in prisons across the nation are overcrowding and extreme physical danger.

32. Subsequent to the settlement of *Ruiz* v. *Estelle*, the unconstitutional conditions in Texas prisons are removed and the Texas prison system emerged as a model correctional enterprise.

33. *Rhodes* v. *Chapman* dealt with the problems of strip searches and solitary confinement.

34. Over the past decade, *Rhodes* v. *Chapman* has resulted in a reduction in the number of cases in which prisoners successfully challenge overcrowding on Eighth Amendment grounds.

35. Increased surveillance and the introduction of new technology to corrections have made inmate uprisings and riots a thing of the past.

ANSWERS TO THE PRACTICE EXAM

1. e	13. d	25. F
2. b	14. b	26. F
3. c	15. b	27. F
4. a	16. b	28. T
5. d	17. a	29. F
6. a	18. b	30. T
7. a	19. c	31. T
8. c	20. a	32. F
9. a	21. T	33. F
10. a	22. F	34. T
11. c	23. F	35. F
12. a	24. T	

CHAPTER 17

Probation, Parole, and Community-Based Correction

CHAPTER OUTLINE

I. Community-Based Correction; intermediate sanctions

II. Criminal Justice Diversion
   A. The removal of offenders from the application of the criminal law at any stage of the police or court process
   B. The development of diversion
      1. informal diversion, past and present
      2. Chicago Boys Court, early example of formalized diversion within the juvenile justice system
      3. New York City's Youth Counsel Bureau (early 1950s)
      4. District of Columbia's Project Crossroads
   C. Patterns of diversion
      1. the criminal justice process as a negative influence on offenders
      2. endorsements of diversion by both the 1967 President's Commission and the 1973 National Advisory Commission
      3. expansion of diversion during the 1970s (LEAA)
      4. youth service bureaus, counseling, tutoring, crisis intervention, etc.
      5. public inebriation programs, use of detoxification centers instead of taking arrested public inebriates to jail
      6. civil commitment, for some drug users, sexual deviants, and mentally ill offenders
      7. citizens dispute settlement, use of mediation to resolve conflict

8. Treatment Alternatives to Street Crime (TASC), bridge between the criminal justice system and the substance abuse treatment system
   D. The impact of diversion- evaluation research is inconclusive
   E. Community service programs

III. Probation
   A. John August, the father of probation
   B. The nature of probation
      1. probation as a sentence (disposition)
      2. probation as a status, a system, and a process
   C. The probation philosophy
      1. nondangerous offenders do not need to be incarcerated for the protection of the community
      2. incarceration can make offenders worse
      3. includes elements of community protection and rehabilitation
      4. pragmatic issues
         a. prison overcrowding
         b. cost of imprisonment
         c. probation as more humane than prison
   D. Suspended sentences and conditional release
      1. withholding the imposition or execution of a court imposed penalty for a period of time dependent on the offender's good behavior
      2. suspension of imposition
      3. suspension of execution
      4. conditional and unconditional discharge
   E. The presentence or probation investigation
      1. probation administered in various ways
      2. presentence investigation, variations by jurisdiction
      3. privately commissioned presentence reports
      4. variations in length and content
      5. studies indicate a high correlation between probation recommendation and actual sentence given by the judge
      6. due process requirement (*Williams* v. *New York*)
   F. Conditions of probation
      1. state laws prohibiting or permitting probation for some offenses
      2. factors which influence the prosecutor's and judge's decisions concerning sentencing
      3. standard conditions of probation
      4. special conditions related to offender's needs, crime, or special circumstances
      5. requirement for payment of supervision fees
      6. conditions of probation are generally considered constitutional; searches governed by *Griffin* v. *Wisconsin* (1987)
   G. Restitution programs
      1. offenders must repay victims for monetary losses resulting from the crime
      2. often used as a condition of probation
      3. rationales for restitution
      4. criticisms of restitution

H. Probation services
   1. the casework approach, diagnosis and treatment
   2. determination of supervision requirements
   3. quality and quantity of treatment services vary
   4. reasons for poor quality probation services
      a. requirements and backgrounds of probation officers vary widely
      b. probation officer apathy
      c. low salaries, limited advancement, low level of career mobility
      d. probation officer attitudes and styles differ considerably (working styles)
I. Shock probation
   1. brief period of incarceration followed by suspension of sentence and probation
   2. arguments in favor of shock probation
   3. arguments against shock probation
   4. evaluation research is inconclusive concerning impact on recidivism
J. Intensive probation supervision
   1. closer surveillance and tighter control than traditional probation
   2. intended to reduce prison crowding and protect society
   3. intensive supervision in Georgia
   4. evaluation research shows mixed and ambiguous results
K. Probation violation and revocation
   1. probation as conditional, not absolute, freedom
   2. new arrest or technical violation can result in revocation
   3. absconding, failing to report as required, a form of escape
   4. discretionary authority of probation officer
   5. only the court can revoke probation
   6. requirement for due process
      a. *Mempa* v. *Rhay* (1967)
      b. *Morrissey* v. *Brewer* (1972)
      c. *Gagnon* v. *Scarpelli* (1973)
L. The effectiveness of probation
   1. probation is the most widely used sanction
   2. research has produced contradictory findings; many probationers are still a threat to the community
   3. effectiveness may vary considerably from one jurisdiction to another

IV. Parole
   A. The dual nature of parole
      1. release process
      2. supervision process
      3. purposes of parole
   B. The origins of parole
      1. Maconochie and Crofton
      2. "good time" laws
      3. Zebulon Brockway and the Elmira Reformatory

C. Parole administration
    1. differences between parole and probation
    2. the parole board
        a. select offenders for parole
        b. provide control and supervision
        c. discharge parolees from supervision
        d. make revocation decisions
    3. American Correctional Association recommendations concerning parole boards
    4. board members differ greatly in experience with the criminal justice system
D. Eligibility for parole
    1. parole is not a right
    2. parole eligibility, earliest date that a inmate can be considered for parole
    3. good time as a factor
    4. the parole hearing
        a. conducted in private
        b. procedures vary
        c. wide discretion
        d. some due process required; Greenholtz case (1979); *Pennsylvania Board of Probation and Parole* v. *Scott*
    5. parole selection
        a. statutory requirements and legislative mandates
        b. prior record
        c. institutional conduct
        d. parole plan
        e. political influences
        f. an informed guess
        g. unpredictability of human behavior
    6. statistical prediction methods
        a. scientific parole prediction
        b. experience tables
        c. problems with parole prediction tables
    7. American Law Institute guidelines
        a. Model Penal Code
        b. Who should *not* be paroled?
    8. mandatory release
        a. prosecutor's recommendation
        b. the role of good time credit
        c. mandatory release, required by statute upon completion of sentence
E. Conditions of parole
    1. what the offender must do and what he may not do
    2. reform conditions and control conditions
    3. special conditions as with probation
    4. some conditions have been ruled unconstitutional in recent years
F. Parole supervision and services
    1. parole officer's duty to supervise, aid, and control parolees

Probation, Parole, and Community-Based Correction 169

        2. parole officers are armed peace officers in some states
        3. the difficulty of supervising parolees leads to a quasi-law enforcement role for the parole officer
    G. Parole violation and revocation
        1. similar to probation
        2. due process requirements; *Morrissey* v. *Brewer*
        3. disagreement over how long the parolee must serve in prison after revocation
        4. "street time" and "dead time"
    H. Parole discharge
        1. "max out", reach maximum expiration date
        2. discharged by parole board prior to maximum expiration date; executive clemency
        3. pardon by the governor

V. Trends in Community-Based Correction
    A. Increasing use of community correction, especially for non-violent offenders
    B. Furlough and temporary release
        1. furlough, authorized, unescorted absence from prison for a specified time period
        2. home furlough as a means of preparing an inmate for release
        3. work release, inmate is allowed out of prison to work for pay in the local community
        4. study release; similar to work release, but for academic or vocational education
        5. experiences with temporary release
            a. criticisms
            b. the problem of offenders committing new crimes
            c. absconding
            d. risks probably limit wide public acceptance
            e. halfway houses and prerelease centers
    C. Should parole be abolished?
        1. criticisms of parole
            a. unstructured decision-making
            b. parole tasks are beyond our capabilities
            c. we cannot predict future human behavior
            d. increases sentence disparity
        2. various theories of the parolee's status
        3. some states have abolished parole
        4. little effect on recidivism

VI. Summary

REVIEW OF KEY TERMS, CONCEPTS, AND IDEAS

Write the definitions for the key terms in the space provided.

    1. community-based correction—_____
_____

Chapter 17

2. diversion—

3. furlough—

4. *Gagnon* v. *Scarpelli*—

5. good time—

6. intensive probation supervision—

7. intermediate sanctions—

8. mandatory release—

9. maximum expiration date—

10. *Mempa* v. *Rhay*—

11. *Morrissey* v. *Brewer*—

12. parole —

13. parole prediction—

14. *Pennsylvania Board of Probation and Parole* v. *Scott*—

15. probation—

16. restitution—

17. shock probation—_____

18. suspended sentence—_____

19. *Williams v. New York*—_____

DISCUSSION

You are an adult probation officer in your home county. You have just completed the following presentence report. Based on what you have learned about the defendant, you must now make a sentencing recommendation to Judge I.L. Hangem. You may recommend one of the following:

A. Defer formal sentencing and place the defendant in a diversion program for six (6) months. If he is drug-free and crime-free at the end of this period, close the case with no further action.
B. Fine the defendant $500.00.
C. Place the defendant on probation for one (1) year.
D. Sentence the defendant to six (6) months in the county jail.

After you make your sentencing recommendation, write a one-page essay explaining why you made this recommendation.

PRESENTENCE REPORT
DEFENDANT: RICKY ROE

OFFENSE: MISDEMEANOR POSSESSION OF MARIJUANA

A. Legal Record
 1. Present Offense: The defendant is an 18 year old, white, single male who is a senior at Our Town High School. Mr. Roe pleaded guilty to a misdemeanor charge of possession of marijuana. On 4-30-01, he was observed by Officer John Law (the police department school liaison officer) to be in possession of a quantity of marijuana while on school grounds. Mr. Roe states that the marijuana was for his personal use, and that he had no intention of trying to sell to anyone. He was unable to identify the person from whom he purchased the marijuana. He appeared candid during my interview with him, and seems to be worried about the outcome of his case.
 2. Prior Record: The defendant was referred to juvenile court by school officials when he was 14 years old for truancy. He was given a warning by the juvenile court judge and has had a good school attendance record since that time. At age 16, Mr. Roe was taken into custody by city police for minor possession of alcohol. He was released to the custody of his mother.
B. Family and Personal History: Mr. Roe is an only child. His parents are divorced. He lives with his mother, and his father lives in Colorado. He has lived with his mother at his present address for ten (10) years. His grandparents live in this county, and he often spends weekends with them on their

farm. The defendant likes to fish and has played organized baseball for the past several summers with a local team. Schoolmates report that he sometimes loses his temper over minor things. A couple of students said that they were afraid that he might become violent at some point, but there is no indication that he has ever bullied, attacked, or threatened anyone. Mr. Roe's mother works two jobs and often does not get home until after 9:00 PM. Her income is around $22,000.00 a year. The defendant works at Food World after school as a stocker/bagger, and usually gets home around 7:00 PM.

C. Education: The school principal reports that the defendant is an average student who should graduate on time. He played in the marching band in the 10th and 11th grades, but apparently lost interest and dropped out. He has not given the teachers any trouble, and is not involved in any clubs, sports, or other school activities. Mr. Roe says he wants to attend vocational school after graduation to study electronics and computer repair.

D. Drug and Alcohol Use: The defendant began consuming beer at age 12. He would take a couple of cans of beer from his grandfather's refrigerator on weekends without his grandfather's knowledge. The defendant stated that he started experimenting with marijuana at age 14. According to him, he smokes not more than one joint a day, except sometimes on weekends. Mr. Roe occasionally consumes alcohol, usually while partying with friends on weekends. He says that he gets drunk sometimes, but hates the hangover. He also smokes cigarettes at the rate of about a pack a day. The defendant strongly denies that he has ever used hard drugs, which he says are for "losers".

E. Summary: Mr. Roe has never been in serious trouble. He is concerned about the potential punishment on the present charge, however, and swears that he has learned his lesson. He accepts responsibility for his behavior. The defendant was honest and straightforward during our meetings, and did not try to shift the blame as young persons often do. Although his home-life is less than ideal, he seems to have a good relationship with his mother, and she seems to genuinely care about his welfare.

Sentencing Recommendation: _____

Explanation:

PRACTICE EXAM

The following practice exam should help you as you study the key terms and ideas presented in Chapter 17.

MULTIPLE CHOICE

1. _____ is a preadjudication disposition.
    a. Diversion
    b. Probation
    c. Parole
    d. Community-based correction

2. Many social scientists argue in favor of diversion programs because
   a. they reduce court backlog.
   b. they reduce the costs of criminal processing.
   c. although the purpose of the criminal justice process is to protect society, it often contributes to the very behavior it is trying to eliminate.
   d. all of the above.

3. Probation is
   a. a sentence.
   b. a status.
   c. a process.
   d. all of the above.

4. Which of the following is an incorrect statement regarding presentence investigation reports?
   a. There is a high correlation between a probation officer's recommendation and the judge's sentence.
   b. They generally include the characteristics of the offender, an evaluative summary, and a recommendation.
   c. They are fairly standard in their depth and content in jurisdictions across the United States.
   d. All of the above.

5. Recent court decisions have affirmed the correctness of such conditions of probation as
   a. that the probationer must abstain from the use of alcohol.
   b. that the probationer must make payment of restitution.
   c. that the probationer must attend a drug treatment program.
   d. all of the above.

6. Restitution has been criticized on the grounds that
   a. payments go to the victim rather than the state.
   b. it can be a punitive sanction rather than a rehabilitative one.
   c. it increases the cost of judicial processing.
   d. it serves no useful purpose.

7. The immediate result of a probation violation is
   a. revocation of probation.
   b. a sentence of imprisonment.
   c. a decision by the probation officer as to whether the probationer should be cited for violation.
   d. a violation hearing.

8. In _____ it was held that a probationer had a constitutional right to counsel at any revocation proceeding where the imposition of sentence had been suspended but would be enjoined following revocation.
   a. *Mempa* v. *Rhay*
   b. *Menechino* v. *Oswald*
   c. *Kramer* v. *Kramer*
   d. *Morrissey* v. *Brewer*

9. The decision in *Morrissey* v. *Brewer* dealt with
   a. the right to counsel at probation revocation hearings.
   b. due process requirements at parole revocation hearings.
   c. the content of preparole reports as they affected paroling decisions.
   d. probation officers' recommendations regarding revocation.

10. Parole selection decisions are usually based on
    a. common sense and intuition.
    b. educated guess and hunch.
    c. scientific prediction methods.
    d. all of the above.

11. A parolee's "date of delinquency" refers to
    a. the date of arrest on the original charge.
    b. the date of sentence on the original charge.
    c. the date of release on parole.
    d. the point at which the violation occurred.

12. The least effective of the community-based correctional programs is
    a. probation.
    b. the furlough.
    c. the halfway house.
    d. a, b, and c above all have their problems and it would be difficult to tell.

13. In *Greenholtz* v. *Inmates of Nebraska Penal and Correctional Complex* the U.S. Supreme Court affirmed previous decisions that
    a. prisoners should be paroled when it is believed that their behavior will not be incompatible with the welfare of the community.
    b. parole hearings need not have all the elements of due process as required at criminal trials.
    c. parolees do not have "present private interests" that require protection.
    d. probation revocation must not be a capricious decision based on age, sex, or racial or religious biases.

14. The decision to grant parole is made by
    a. parole officers.
    b. county parole boards.
    c. state or federal parole boards.
    d. the sentencing court.

15. In parole jargon, _____ refers to time served on the street after date of a parole violation.
    a. "street time"
    b. "delinquent time"
    c. "bad time"
    d. "dead time"

TRUE/FALSE

16. Community-based correction refers to activities and programs of a rehabilitative nature that have effective ties with the local government.

17. Under formal court diversion programs, discretionary decisions are made by police and prosecutors to suspend the criminal process.

18. In *Gardner* v. *Florida*, the Court ruled that probation departments cannot collect fees from probationers to pay for the cost of their supervision.

19. Civil commitment programs are based on a medical model of rehabilitation.

20. With respect to conditions of probation, the courts have generally agreed that conditions are unconstitutional when they bear no reasonable relationship to the crime committed or to the defendant's probationary status.

21. Technical violations of probation involve arrests for new crimes.

22. Parole prediction tables are accurate in indicating the best parole risks.

23. Senator Edward Kennedy has recently argued for the abolition of parole on the grounds that it compounds sentencing disparities.

24. According to the Rand study of probation effectiveness, most offenders do fairly well on probation.

25. According to data published by the Bureau of Justice Statistics, the average length of stay in prison is 3 years or less.

26. The Treatment Alternatives to Street Crime program was quickly abandoned due to lack of state and local support.

27. The Oklahoma Preparole Conditional Supervision Program is a regular part of the state's correctional process, and allows prisoners to leave the penitentiary, under strict supervision, before they are eligible for regular parole.

28. Good time refers to the number of days deducted from a sentence for good behavior, meritorious service, particular kinds of work, or other considerations.

FILL IN THE BLANK

29. The "father of probation" was _____.

30. _____ refers to the practice of incarcerating the offender for a brief period of time, and then suspending the remainder of the sentence and placing the offender on probation.

Chapter 17

31. Only the _____ has the authority to revoke probation.

32. The word "parole" comes from the French, meaning _____.

33. Among the first diversion programs in the United States was _____.

ANSWERS TO THE PRACTICE EXAM

1. a	12. d	23. T
2. c	13. b	24. F
3. d	14. c	25. T
4. c	15. d	26. F
5. d	16. T	27. T
6. b	17. F	28. T
7. c	18. F	29. John Augustus
8. a	19. T	30. Shock probation
9. b	20. T	31. court
10. d	21. F	32. "word of honor"
11. d	22. F	33. the Chicago Boys Court

CHAPTER 18

Juvenile Justice: An Overview

CHAPTER OUTLINE

I. The Nature of Juvenile Justice
   A. Who is an adult? Who is a juvenile?
      1. the "magic number"
      2. the "special status" of juveniles
      3. the philosophy of protecting and correcting children
   B. The juvenile and the juvenile court
      1. violation of the criminal law
      2. status offense
      3. victim of abuse or neglect
   C. Purpose of juvenile sanctions
      1. sentencing philosophies in criminal (adult) court
      2. juvenile court, "in the best interests of the child"
   D. The emergence of juvenile justice
      1. the treatment of juveniles in colonial America
      2. the house of refuge
   E. *Parens patriae*
      1. shifting explanations of criminal behavior
      2. *parens patriae*, the state as the parent
      3. crime as a symptom; treating the underlying problem
      4. the "child savers" and the Illinois Juvenile Court Act

F. Modern juvenile courts
   1. some 3000 juvenile courts in the U.S.
   2. jurisdiction and procedures vary
   3. delinquency
   4. delinquent
   5. adjudication

II. The Processing of Juvenile Offenders
   A. Police discretion
      1. informal adjustment
      2. taking a juvenile into custody (arrest)
      3. factors influencing discretion
   B. Petition and intake
      1. petition alleges that the juvenile is a delinquent
      2. intake hearing, a preliminary examination of the facts of the case
      3. the role of the intake officer, alternatives
   C. Detention and bail
      1. detention hearing, release to parent or retain in custody?
      2. objectives of temporary detention
      3. monetary bail is generally not used in juvenile cases
   D. Adjudication and disposition
      1. adjudication inquiry, do the facts and circumstances warrant a formal hearing?
      2. adjudication hearing
         a. civil proceeding
         b. judge presides on behalf of the child
         c. determination of whether the juvenile committed the alleged offenses
      3. disposition hearing
         a. the judge decides how to settle the case
         b. alternative dispositions

III. Juveniles and the Constitution
   A. Juvenile court process as a civil, not criminal process
   B. *Kent* v. *United States* (1966)
   C. Due process and juvenile proceedings
      1. *In re Gault* (1967)
      2. *In re Winship* (1970)
      3. *Breed* v. *Jones* (1975)
      4. *McKeiver* v. *Pennsylvania,* (1971)
   D. Police encounters and juvenile rights
      1. The Uniform Juvenile Court Act
      2. *in loco parentis*
      3. juveniles and the Fourth Amendment
      4. *New Jersey* v. *T.L.O.* (1985)

IV. Critical Issues in Juvenile Justice
   A. Juvenile justice as an imperfect system
   B. Status offenders
      1. PINS, MINS, CHINS, CINS, JINS, and YINS
      2. the movement to decriminalize status offenses
      3. efforts to repeal status offender jurisdiction
      4. The Juvenile Justice and Juvenile Delinquency Prevention Act (1974)
   C. Juveniles in the adult courts
      1. waiver of jurisdiction, transfer of a case from juvenile to criminal court
      2. disagreement among the states
      3. *Kent* v. *United States* (1966), requirement for a waiver hearing with basic due process
      4. protection of the community versus appropriate treatment for the delinquent
   D. Juveniles on death row, *Stanford* v. *Kentucky* (1989)
   E. Juvenile detention
      1. *Schall* v. *Martin* (1984), preventive detention of juveniles permissible in some cases
      2. dangers to juveniles in detention
   F. Juvenile corrections
      1. community-based treatment; diversion
      2. probation, the primary form of community treatment in the juvenile system
      3. correctional institutions

V. Is "Child Saving" Dead?

VI. Summary

REVIEW OF KEY TERMS, CONCEPTS, AND IDEAS

Write the definitions for the key terms in the space provided.

1. adjudication—

2. adjudication hearing—

3. adjudication inquiry—

4. *Breed* v. *Jones*—

5. delinquency—

180 Chapter 18

6. delinquent—

7. detention hearing—

8. disposition hearing—

9. Illinois Juvenile Court Act—

10. *in loco parentis*—

11. *In re Gault*—

12. *In re Winship*—

13. intake hearing—

14. *Kent v. United States*—

15. *McKeiver v. Pennsylvania*—

16. *New Jersey v. T.L.O*—

17. *parens patriae*—

18. petition—

19. *Schall v. Martin*—

20. *Stanford v. Kentucky*—

21. status offenders—_____
   _____

22. status offense—_____
   _____

23. waiver of jurisdiction—_____
   _____

DISCUSSION

The Office of Juvenile Justice and Delinquency Prevention is an agency of the Office of Justice Programs, which in turn is organized under the U.S. Department of Justice. OJJDP maintains an excellent Web site (http://ojjdp.ncjrs.org/) which includes a wealth of information about juveniles, juvenile delinquency, offenders, victims, and case processing. Visit this website, look around, and answer the following questions by linking to "Statistical Briefing Book."

1. How is the juvenile population in the United States expected to change through the year 2015? What is the projection for your state?
2. What was the birth rate for mothers ages 15-17 in your state in the most recent year reported? How has the rate changed in recent years?
3. Juveniles accounted for 16% of all Violent Crime Index arrests and 32% of all Property Crime Index arrests in 1999. What are the percentages for arson, stolen property, and murder?
4. Examine the relationship between juvenile victims and their offenders. What percentage of robberies was committed by non-strangers? Aggravated assaults? Simple assaults?
5. Study the various case flow charts that depict the movement of juvenile offenders through the juvenile justice system. Select a particular offense and record the number of cases out of a "typical" 1,000 that are petitioned and adjudicated. What dispositions come out of these adjudicated cases? How do the outcomes of petitioned cases compare to non-petitioned cases?
6. What is the difference between "detention" and "commitment"? What is the approximate commitment rate in your state? What is the approximate detention rate? Explain the difference between these rates.

PRACTICE EXAM

Take the following practice exam; it will help you to review some of the main ideas covered in Chapter 18.

MULTIPLE CHOICE

1. In juvenile proceedings, a(n) _____ is the stage in which a judge presides on behalf of the child to determine if he or she actually committed the alleged offense.
   a. waiver
   b. disposition
   c. adjudication
   d. conviction or acquittal

2. Perhaps the major difference between the adult and juvenile justice systems involves the
   a. types of crimes juveniles commit.
   b. nature and purpose of the sanctions imposed.
   c. length of sentences imposed.
   d. the number of stages in the disposition process.

3. The first systematic attempt to separate juvenile offenders from adult criminals in correctional settings occurred at the
   a. Chicago Boys Court
   b. New York Youth Council Bureau
   c. House of Refuge
   d. Illinois Juvenile Court

4. Under the *parens patriae* philosophy of court intervention, the intention is to
   a. diagnose the problem and prescribe the appropriate treatment.
   b. permit an informal court process unhampered by the requirements of official criminal procedure.
   c. protect the future of the youth.
   d. all of the above.

5. Juvenile court processing is best described as a _____ procedure.
   a. criminal
   b. civil
   c. chancery
   d. adversary

6. The "child savers" were
   a. welfare workers who ran missions and soup kitchens for New York's thousands of street waifs.
   b. the legislators who hammered out the *parens patriae* philosophy into workable juvenile procedure.
   c. the reformers who advocated the structuring of a juvenile justice system.
   d. the disciplinarians in the house of refuge.

7. In _____ juvenile courts, all proceedings occur in the state's family or domestic relations courts.
   a. coordinated
   b. designated
   c. autonomous
   d. dichotomous

8. Which of the following does *not* occur at an intake hearing in a juvenile case?
   a. probable cause for the petition
   b. evaluation of the evidence
   c. plea negotiation
   d. background investigation of the youth

9. Proof "beyond a reasonable doubt" became a requirement for an adjudication of delinquency as a result of
   a. *In re Gault.*
   b. *Breed* v. *Jones.*
   c. *Kent* v. *United States.*
   d. *In re Winship.*

10. The ruling in *New Jersey* v. *T.L.O.* dealt with a _____ Amendment issue.
    a. Fourth
    b. Fifth
    c. Sixth
    d. Fourteenth

TRUE/FALSE

11. In the United States, juveniles are held to an alternative standard of behavior because of their "special status" of being below the age of majority.

12. Truancy, curfew violations, and vandalism are all examples of status offenses.

13. The juvenile court process and juvenile court sanctions, at least in theory, are based on a rehabilitative model.

14. The "child savers" movement crystallized in the passage of the Illinois Juvenile Court Act in 1899.

15. One of the most notable aspects of the Scottish juvenile justice system is its propensity to sentence juvenile offenders to incarceration.

16. Police officers have considerable discretion in street encounters with juveniles.

17. At the intake hearing in juvenile proceedings, a judge conducts a preliminary examination into the facts of the case.

18. Juvenile court proceedings, at the adjudication stage, are closed to the public.

19. The Supreme Court has not ruled specifically on the applicability of the *Miranda* safeguards to the juvenile process.

20. The Supreme Court has remained silent on the issue of juveniles on death row.

FILL IN THE BLANK

21. A _____ is an act declared by statute to be a crime because it violates the standards of behavior expected of children.

22. _____ represented the first Supreme Court evaluation of the constitutionality of juvenile court proceedings.

23. Under the philosophy of _____ the state takes over the role of parent.

24. _____ involves criminal law violations that would be considered "crimes" if committed by an adult.

25. Running away is an example of a _____ offense.

26. In juvenile proceedings, a _____ is a document alleging that a youth is a delinquent or status offender and requesting the juvenile court to assume jurisdiction.

27. In *Breed* v. *Jones*, the protection against _____ was extended to juvenile cases.

28. The Juvenile Justice and Juvenile Delinquency Act required the _____ of status offenders by 1985.

29. A _____ of jurisdiction sends a juvenile to an adult court for criminal processing.

30. The issue in *Schall* v. *Martin* was the _____ of juveniles.

ANSWERS TO THE PRACTICE EXAM

1. c	11. T	21. status offense
2. b	12. F	22. *Kent* v. *United States*
3. c	13. T	23. *parens patriae*
4. d	14. T	24. Delinquency
5. b	15. T	25. status
6. c	16. T	26. petition
7. a	17. F	27. double jeopardy
8. c	18. T	28. deinstitutionalization
9. d	19. T	29. waiver
10. a	20. F	30. preventive detention

Harcourt College Publishers

Where Learning Comes to Life

TECHNOLOGY

Technology is changing the learning experience, by increasing the power of your textbook and other learning materials; by allowing you to access more information, more quickly; and by bringing a wider array of choices in your course and content information sources.

Harcourt College Publishers has developed the most comprehensive Web sites, e-books, and electronic learning materials on the market to help you use technology to achieve your goals.

PARTNERS IN LEARNING

Harcourt partners with other companies to make technology work for you and to supply the learning resources you want and need. More importantly, Harcourt and its partners provide avenues to help you reduce your research time of numerous information sources.

Harcourt College Publishers and its partners offer increased opportunities to enhance your learning resources and address your learning style. With quick access to chapter-specific Web sites and e-books . . . from interactive study materials to quizzing, testing, and career advice . . . Harcourt and its partners bring learning to life.

Harcourt's partnership with Digital:Convergence™ brings :CRQ™ technology and the :CueCat™ reader to you and allows Harcourt to provide you with a complete and dynamic list of resources designed to help you achieve your learning goals. Just swipe the cue to view a list of Harcourt's partners and Harcourt's print and electronic learning solutions.

http://www.harcourtcollege.com/partners/